THE BIRDS

Other English versions by Dudley Fitts

THE LYSISTRATA OF ARISTOPHANES
THE FROGS OF ARISTOPHANES

By Dudley Fitts and Robert Fitzgerald

THE ALCESTIS OF EURIPIDES
THE ANTIGONE OF SOPHOCLES
THE OEDIPUS REX OF SOPHOCLES

ARISTOPHANES

THE BIRDS

AN ENGLISH VERSION
BY DUDLEY FITTS

HARCOURT, BRACE AND COMPANY

NEW YORK

PA
3877
A8
1957

for ROBERT FITZGERALD

ALASTOR. *Sed quid opus est triremi?* CHARON. *Nichil, si velim in mediâ palude rursus naufragium facere.* ALASTOR. *Ob multitudinem?* CHARON. *Scilicet.* ALASTOR. *Atqui umbras vehis, non corpora. Quantulum autem ponderis habent umbrae?* CHARON. *Sint tipulae, tamen tipularum tanta vis esse potest, ut onerent cymbam. Tum scis et cymbam umbratilem esse.*

INTRODUCTORY NOTE

The Birds was produced at the feast of the Great Dionysia of 414 B.C., and although it is certainly the most fanciful and one of the most lyrical of Aristophanes' plays, it won only the second prize. Composed during those tense months after the sailing of the Sicilian Expedition, when the disheartening war must have seemed endless in prospect and even victory a sick delusion, it is nevertheless not a war play. It is outspoken enough, particularly in its attacks upon the kind of civil neurosis that finds traitors and enemy agents in every office and that encourages, applauds and rewards the professional informer; but the attack this time is of less importance than the creation of a comic dream, the dream of Cloudcuckooland the Beautiful, that ideal commonwealth in the skies. Elaborate political reconstructions of the dream have been made—classical scholarship is ingenious and tireless—but they seem, in all their complexity, pastimes better suited to the academies of Cloudcuckooland itself than to the enrichment of our understanding. *The Birds* is not a play of escape: it is too honestly aware of its time for that; but it is primarily an entertainment, and as such, I think, it should be read and weighed.

For the *rationale* of my translation I must refer those interested to my remarks prefatory to *Lysistrata* and *The Frogs*. In general, however, I hope that I have reduced the number of liberties that were conscious on my part, and that my ignorance, not my arrogance, is to blame for the errors. At the same time, I demand a certain licence in rendering the choral passages and in handling mythological or topical references. Many difficulties can be taken care of in the Notes; but there are times when only a loose paraphrase, or maybe the incorporation of explanatory ideas into the text itself, can save the poem. And it is my faith that the poem is what matters most.

The text followed is the Budé, established by Coulon, and the lineation indicated at the top of each page is in agreement with this. In the distribution of a few speeches I have preferred the reading of other editors, and have sometimes relied upon otherwise unreliable MSS. sources because they made better theatre sense. Once or twice I have followed myself alone, so amorous is *hybris*, and assigned a speech or two as it has never been assigned before.

For many corrections and the best of suggestions I am indebted to my colleague Alston Hurd Chase, and to the poet and Hellenist to whom this translation is dedicated.

DF

CONTENTS

PERSONS REPRESENTED:

EUELPIDES

PISTHETAIROS

A BIRD SERVANT

EPOPS

CHORUS OF BIRDS

A PRIEST

A POET

A TRAVELLING PROPHET

METON

AN INSPECTOR

A DECREE-VENDOR

THREE MESSENGERS

IRIS

A HERALD

A PARRICIDE

KINESIAS

AN INFORMER

PROMETHEUS

POSEIDON

A TRIBALLIAN GOD

HERAKLES

The supernumeraries include various servants and liturgical attendants, PROKNE the Nightingale wife of EPOPS, MANES a slave, and BASILEIA the bride of PISTHETAIROS.

PROLOGUE

[*A waste region. Rocks, low bushes, a few thin trees.
In the background, a steep rock face surmounted by a
single tree. Enter two old men,* PISTHETAIROS *and* EUEL-
PIDES, *followed by slaves carrying baggage.* PISTHETAI-
ROS *has a raven perched upon his wrist;* EUELPIDES *has
a jackdaw. Weariness and frustration.*

EUELPIDES [*to the jackdaw*]:
  Straight ahead? Over by that tree?
PISTHETAIROS [*to the raven*]:

                              Oh, damn your feathers!
  —Euelpidês, this fool fowl keeps cawing
  a retreat.
EUELPIDES:
                    I know. What's the use?
  All this humping up and down hills,
  we'll be wrecks before we find the right road.
PISTHETAIROS:
  Miles and miles, walking around in circles,
  all because of a brainless bird.
EUELPIDES:

                              Yes,
  tramping my toenails off for a damned jackdaw.
PISTHETAIROS:
  I wonder where we are.
EUELPIDES:

                    Do you think we could find our way back?

PISTHETAIROS:

Exekestidês himself couldn't find his way back.

EUELPIDES:

Hell!

PISTHETAIROS:

That's a road you'll have to go on your own.

EUELPIDES:

No, damn it, but I was thinking of that birdseller.
Nice service that was,
swearing that these two specimens would lead us straight
to Tereus, the king who turned into a Hoopoe;
selling us a jackdaw for a penny, the damned jackass,
and three pennies for that raven. What a pair!
All they can do is peck.

[*To the jackdaw:*

—What's the matter now?
Forgotten how to shut your beak? Or a brilliant thought
like leading us bang up against that rock?
I don't see any road.

PISTHETAIROS:

Not so much as a path.

EUELPIDES:

Do you think that raven of yours is still conscious?

PISTHETAIROS:

I don't know. He sort of grunts, every once in a while.

4

EUELPIDES:

I mean, do you think he knows what he's up to?

PISTHETAIROS:

He seems to know enough to chew on my finger.

EUELPIDES:

Silly, isn't it?
Here we are, two of us for the birds,
and we can't even find the road.

[Addresses the audience:

—Gentlemen:
Our trouble's just the reverse of Sakas's.
He isn't a citizen, and he's dying to become one;
but we,
native born, pure strain, citizens all our lives,
we can't get away from Athens fast enough.
Not that we don't like Athens:
it's a fine city, progressive, full of opportunities
to appear in court, citizens
happy as locusts droning in the shade—
only I must say they seem to do most of their droning
before a judge.
To come right down to it,
that's why the two of us are taking this walk,
fitted out with baskets and braziers and myrtle boughs.
We're looking for a less strenuous residence,
a City where we can pass our lives in peace;

and we thought of Tereus:
what with all the flying he's done, maybe
he'll know a nice restricted—

PISTHETAIROS:

Look! Look!

EUELPIDES:

What's the matter?

PISTHETAIROS:

The rock! Look at my raven!

EUELPIDES:

Yes, and my jackdaw sees something: his beak's
open again. I'll give you odds
there's birds around that rock. Let's do something.

PISTHETAIROS:

Why don't you go bang your foot against that rock?

EUELPIDES:

You go bang your head. It'll make twice the noise.

PISTHETAIROS:

Pick up a stone and knock.

EUELPIDES:

Anything you say.

—Porter! Porter!

PISTHETAIROS:

Idiot, that's no way
to call a Hoopoe. You should say "Hoop! Hoop!"

EUELPIDES:

Hoop! Hoop!

6

He's just had a lunch of ant and myrtle salad,
and now it's time for his nap.

EUELPIDES:

Bother his nap!

SERVANT:

He won't like this a bit. But if you say so,
I'll do it. It's no skin off my beak.

PISTHETAIROS:

Get going!

[*Exit* SERVANT

To hell with him and that chasm he calls a beak!

EUELPIDES:

He scared away my jackdaw.

PISTHETAIROS:

You got scared,
you mean, and let it loose.

EUELPIDES:

How about you?
When you were falling flat on your face over there,
didn't you let your raven fly away?

PISTHETAIROS:

I certainly did not.

EUELPIDES:

Then where is it?

PISTHETAIROS:

Absent.

9

EUELPIDES:

You can wash your hands of it now, old lion-heart.

EPOPS [*within*]:

Open the door. I'm going out to meet them.

[*Enter* EPOPS, *the Hoopoe. He is inadequately covered
by thin drooping feathers, and wears a mask with a very
long pointed beak and a tall radiant crest.*

EUELPIDES:

What in the name of High Heraklês is that?
Those feathers! That tiara!

EPOPS:

Gentlemen,
your names, if you please? The purpose of your visit?

EUELPIDES:

The Twelve Gods seem to have visited something, friend,
on you.

EPOPS:

You find my feathers laughable?
Remember: once I was a man.

EUELPIDES:

We are not laughing at you.

EPOPS:

At what, then?

EUELPIDES:

That damned funny beak of yours.

10

EPOPS:

I can't help it. It's Sophoklês' fault,
the way he misrepresented me in his plays.

EUELPIDES:

You are really Tereus? A bird, or a parody?

EPOPS:

Every inch a bird.

EUELPIDES:

What's the matter with your wings?

EPOPS:

Feathers missing.

EUELPIDES:

Some bird disease, or what?

EPOPS:

Every bird moults in the wintertime.
We get new feathers in the spring.

—But tell me:

who are you two?

EUELPIDES:

Mortal men.

EPOPS:

Nationality?

EUELPIDES:

Land of the Free. Home of the Brave.

EPOPS:

I suppose

you're jurymen?

EUELPIDES:

No; you might call us *de*

jure men.

EPOPS:

Isn't that a new crop down there?

EUELPIDES:

If you work hard enough you can grow it in some fields.

EPOPS:

Well, well.—But what brings you to this place?

EUELPIDES:

We want to integrate ourselves with you.

EPOPS:

Why?

EUELPIDES:

Because you were a man once, like us;
because you owed money, like us, and because,
like us, you hated to pay it. Now you are a bird,
with a bird's-eye view of things and a man's knowledge
of all lands under the sun, of every sea.
So we have come to you
as to an authority, meaning no disrespect,
to ask if you can tell us where to find
a soft snug woolly city
where a man can loaf and stretch and lie down in peace.

EPOPS:

A nobler city than Kranaos' town?

EUELPIDES:

Not nobler, no; but something more to our taste.

EPOPS:

More aristocratic?

EUELPIDES:

The Social Register

pains me in a spot I needn't describe.

EPOPS:

What sort of city?

EUELPIDES:

What I have in mind

is a place where the worst of your troubles would be
friends crowding in early in the morning
with invitations: 'Look, Euelpidês,
'I'm giving a dinner today. For God's sake,
'get a bath somewhere, pick up your wife and kids,
'come early and stay late. If you forget,
'I'll never turn to you when I need a friend.'

EPOPS:

I can see that you're fond of troubles.

—How about you?

PISTHETAIROS:

I feel the same way he does.

EPOPS:

For example?

PISTHETAIROS:

I'd like to live in a town

where a friend of mine, father of a goodlooking boy,
would meet me and, 'You old bastard,' he'd say,
'what's this I hear about you from that son of mine?
'He tells me he ran into you outside the gymnasium,
'and though he was fresh from his bath
'you didn't say anything nice to him, or kiss him,
'or feel his balls or his biceps—
'Why, I thought you were a friend of the family!'

EPOPS:

It's clear that both of you want to live the hard life.
Well, this city of yours
does exist, after all. You'll find it on the Red Sea.

EUELPIDES:

And have the *Salaminia* turn up some morning
with a constable on board? Thanks, no sea for us!
Haven't you a Greek city you can recommend?

EPOPS:

How about Lepreon?

EUELPIDES:

                        No. I've never been there,
but the name reminds me of Melanthios.

EPOPS:

Then there's Opoûs, over in Lokris.

EUELPIDES:

                                    No.
You couldn't pay me enough to be Opountios.

14

PISTHETAIROS:

That's the birds' sphere.

EPOPS:

Sphere? What do you mean?

PISTHETAIROS:

It's a space, really; but it revolves,
and everything passes through it, so we scientists
call it a sphere.

Very well. You settle this sphere,
build walls around it, and you'll have a city.
And what's more,
you can lord it over the human race as though
they were so many grasshoppers. And the gods—
why, you can starve them out like the Mêlians.

EPOPS:

How?

PISTHETAIROS:

Just as we manage these things on earth.
Suppose a man wants to consult the Oracle
at Delphoi: well, he has to get a pass
from the Boiotians, because Boiotia's on the way
to the Shrine. And so it will be with the gods:
there's all that air between earth and the top of Olympos,
so if they won't pay tribute to the Birds
you can make it illegal
for the smoke of offering to pass up to them.

EPOPS:

Oh by Earth, by Nets, by Traps, by Springes,
I never heard a cleverer idea in my life!
With you to help me, I will build that city—
that is, if we can get the other Birds to agree.

PISTHETAIROS:

Who will explain it to them?

EPOPS:

You.

I've lived with them so long that they have learned
to speak Man now instead of twittering.

PISTHETAIROS:

Can you call an Assembly?

EPOPS:

Nothing easier.
I'll just step back into the coppice here
and wake my darling wife, my Nightingale.
We'll summon them, she and I,
and they'll come racing when they hear our voices.

PISTHETAIROS:

Oh do, do! Dear Tereus, be quick!
Into the woods, wake the Nightingale!

[*Exit* EPOPS; *presently his voice is heard singing within:*

EPOPS:

Awake, Love, lazy sleeper,
Awake, and pour

18

The lilting glory of your golden throat
For Itys, ours no more.
    Ah, the liquid trill
        Of the holy monody rising
To God's house from the stillness of the woods!
        Phoibos himself, that high
Singer, struck by your music, would sweep
The lutestrings with his delicate fingers
    Antiphonal, and all the air along
        Lead the quiring
Of the tireless gods responsive to your song.

EUELPIDES:

Heavenly God, what a voice that little bird has!
He is drowning the forest with honey.

PISTHETAIROS:

You!

EUELPIDES:

    What?

PISTHETAIROS:

      Be quiet, can't you?

EUELPIDES:

            Why?

PISTHETAIROS:

The Hoopoe is going to sing for us again.

    [*During the following monody, birdcalls are heard
    from various points behind the scene, distant and un-*

certain at first, but increasing in volume and in urgency
until the CHORUS OF BIRDS *enters for the* Párodos.

EPOPS [*within*]:
Epopoí

   popoì epopopoí
  popoì
     iô

 iô

  iô

     To me,

   to
me here, here, here, O
  friends, O feathery
myriads!

     Leave your
fields now, furrows
     deep
  in seed, beak-
wielders,

     swift
  spiralers,

     melodists
of delight
  tíotiotíotì
   All you
divers for stingvoiced gnats

20

[*The* CHORUS *is composed of twenty-six persons dressed in stylized representation of various birds, each with a large beak-mask. These enter separately from every direction, gathering about their leader, the* Flamingo, *in the* orchestra. *The entrance should be complete by the end of the* Hoopoe's *catalogue.*

A BIRD:

Torotìx torotíx.

PISTHETAIROS:

Look, there's one coming now!

EUELPIDES:

What do you suppose it is? A peacock, maybe?

PISTHETAIROS:

The Hoopoe can tell us.

—What kind of bird is that?

EPOPS:

That, Sir, is a water bird; you don't see
that sort every day.

EUELPIDES:

Nice colour; flame-y.

EPOPS:

Naturally. He's a Flamingo.

EUELPIDES:

Oh look!

PISTHETAIROS:

Now what?

25

EUELPIDES:

Another bird.

PISTHETAIROS:

I should say so!

He's a weird sister, all right, as the poet puts it.

See how he struts! I wonder what he is.

EPOPS:

We call him the Bird of Araby.

PISTHETAIROS:

Araby?

Did he come on a flying camel?

EUELPIDES:

There's another one!

By Poseidôn, he looks as if he had been dyed!

PISTHETAIROS:

This is astonishing. Do you mean to say

there's more than one Hoopoe in the world?

EPOPS:

He's the son of Philoklês and a lady Hoopoe,

and I am his grandfather. It's like the formula

'Kallias : Hipponikos :: Hipponikos : Kallias II'.

EUELPIDES:

So that's Kallias II. I see he's losing his feathers.

EPOPS:

A man about town, you know, always getting plucked

by parasites and party girls feathering their own nests.

26

PISTHETAIROS:

Here comes one with a crest. What's he called?

EPOPS:

That one? Gobbler.

EUELPIDES:

I thought Kleonymos was the Gobbler.

PISTHETAIROS:

This can't be Kleonymos: he hasn't thrown away
his crest.

EUELPIDES:

Speaking of that, why do birds
wear crests? To compete in the Armed Men's Race?

EPOPS:

It's like the Karians: crests make fighting safer.

PISTHETAIROS:

I never saw so many birds! They make me nervous.

EUELPIDES:

You said it.
When they lift their wings you can't see where you're going.

EPOPS:

That's the Partridge; and that's—let's see—that one's
the Francolin; the Egyptian Mallard; and that female's
a Hen Kingfisher.

PISTHETAIROS:

What's that in back of her?

EPOPS:

A Shavetail, of course.

27

PISTHETAIROS:

Do birds shave tails?

EPOPS:

Doesn't Sporgilos?

—And that's a female

Owl.

EUELPIDES:

That's an idea! Bringing Owls to Athens.

EPOPS:

Magpie. Turtledove. Lark. Warbler. Spryneck.

Pigeon. Snirt. Falcon. Ringdove. Cuckoo.

Redleg. Firepate. Purple Hatch. Kestrel.

Grebe. Bunting. Lämmergeier. Woodpecker.

PISTHETAIROS:

Birds and more birds!

EUELPIDES:

Even white Blackbirds!

PISTHETAIROS:

The way they chatter and screech at each other!

EUELPIDES:

Do you think they're dangerous?

PISTHETAIROS:

Their beaks are wide open,

and they're certainly looking hard at both of us.

EUELPIDES:

I think so, too.

28

CHORAGOS:

                 Who-oo-oo called this Assembly?
Where is he?

EPOPS:

               Here I am, your tried
and trusted old friend.

CHORAGOS:

                Spea-pea-pea-peak:
What clever new message have you to give us?

EPOPS:

A profitable one, safe, correct, ingenious.
These two gentlemen, both of them keen thinkers,
came here looking for me.

CHORAGOS:

                 Looking for you? Why?

EPOPS:

I am telling you.

          —These elegant old men
have detached themselves temporarily from
the human race and brought us what I am sure
is a plan of promising proportions.

CHORAGOS:

                I think
you have made the greatest blunder in history
What are you talking about?

EPOPS:

               Be not afraid.

CHORAGOS:

Why not?

What have you done to us?

EPOPS:

I have lent an ear
to two respectable bird-struck Senators.

CHORAGOS:

You have?

EPOPS:

I have. And I am proud of it.

CHORAGOS:

What, in our house?

EPOPS:

As sure as I'm standing here.

CHORUS:

Oh misery!   [STROPHE
Duplicity!
Oh horror without end!
Who lays the snare
And leaves us there?
Our old familiar friend!
Is this the Hoopoe of our heart,
Copartner of our fields and skies,
Who bids our ancient laws depart
And sells us to our enemies?

30

CHORAGOS:

We can take care of him later. Just now
it's a matter of these two old fools. Look at them!
The usual penalty is clearly in order:
death by dissection.

PISTHETAIROS:

Done for, by God Almighty!

EUELPIDES:

Your fault, your fault entirely. Why did you ever
lead me here?

PISTHETAIROS:

So that you could follow me.

EUELPIDES:

It's blood and tears for us!

PISTHETAIROS:

Hardly tears for you,
once the Birds have pecked out both your eyes.

CHORUS:

The cock-trump sings.   [ANTISTROPHE
Advance both wings,
O army of the air!
The hour has struck
That ends the luck
Of this repulsive pair.
No clouds that cluster in the sky,
No raindark mountain peaks,

31

Shall save them from the battery
Of our insulted beaks.

CHORAGOS:

Forward! Peck them apart! Flay them!

—Where's

that Wing Commander? Tell him to get moving
on the right!

> [*Immense confusion of movement among the Birds in
> the* orchestra. EUELPIDES *and* PISTHETAIROS *confer apart.*

EUELPIDES:

That settles that.

How do we get out of this mess?

PISTHETAIROS:

Why not

stick around?

EUELPIDES:

Of course. And get pulled apart?

PISTHETAIROS:

I suppose you have figured out some way of escape?

EUELPIDES:

You know I haven't.

PISTHETAIROS:

Then listen to me.

Let them come on. We'll stand here and fight them
with these kitchen pots.

EUELPIDES:

Pots? What good are pots?

PISTHETAIROS:

They'll keep the Owl from attacking us.

EUELPIDES:

How about those fellows with the horrible claws?

PISTHETAIROS:

Stick that spit up in front of you like a spear.

EUELPIDES:

But our eyes?

PISTHETAIROS:

Use a couple of saucers.

EUELPIDES:

What a mind!

You remind me of Nikias. You ought to be
on the General Staff, in charge of secret weapons.

CHORAGOS:

Eleleú!

Ready, beaks at the charge! Let 'em have it!
Grab! Claw! Tear! Gouge! Break the pots first!

[*Much noise on both sides, but no other activity; the
Hoopoe intervenes.*

EPOPS:

Permit me. Just a minute, please.

—With the best intentions,

you are behaving like besotted beasts.

33

What is the good of killing two harmless men,
both of them perfect strangers and, what's more,
related to my wife?

CHORAGOS:

                                Are you promoting
a Be Kind to Wolves week?

EPOPS:

                                Oh, come. I'll admit,
men are our natural enemies; but these men
are different, they really mean us well.
More than that,
they have a practical plan for the good of us all.

CHORAGOS:

A practical plan? Nonsense. Our enemies,
our fathers' enemies—what can they teach us?

EPOPS:

Why, people before this have learned from their enemies.
An open mind's a weapon in itself.
It's not our friends teach us resourcefulness,
but our wise enemies. Cities and princes
have learned the use of warships and fortresses
from necessity, not from friends. Enmity saves
our homes, our children, everything that we love.

CHORAGOS:

You may be right.

                                At least it can do no harm
to hear what they have to say.

34

It may be

we shall take some profit even from what we hate.

[*The Birds cluster in doubtful conference about the*
CHORAGOS.

PISTHETAIROS [*apart to* EUELPIDES]:

They're coming to their senses. Easy, now!

EPOPS [*to the Birds*]:

Think over what I've said. You'll thank me for it.

CHORAGOS:

We have always admired the Hoopoe's intellect.

PISTHETAIROS:

Now we can breathe again.

Leave your pot there on the ground. Pick up your spear—

your spit, I mean—and let's walk around

and see what the place is like.

Keep this side

of the pots, and keep your eye on those Birds. Above all,

don't act as though you were nervous.

EUELPIDES:

I'd like to know:

if they kill us, where'll we get buried?

PISTHETAIROS:

I should hope,

in the National Cemetery. For a first-rate funeral

at the public expense, we'd say we fell gloriously

in combat with the common enemy
at Gettysbird.

[The Birds decide upon a truce.

CHORAGOS:

At ease! Stack arms!
Now we must find out who these strangers are
and what they want.
Listen, Epops!

EPOPS:

I am listening.

CHORAGOS:

Who are these men? Do you know where they are from?

EPOPS:

Travelers from Greece, where education is general.

CHORAGOS:

What brings them to the Birds?

EPOPS:

Ornithophily.
They have heard of your laws and customs and they long
to live with you for ever.

CHORAGOS:

Is it possible?
What else do they say?

EPOPS:

Incredible things, transcending
utterance.

CHORAGOS:

What do they ask from us?
Does 'living with us' mean living as honest friends,
or serving their own interests at our cost?

EPOPS:

This savant speaks of benefits to you
that fairly rob me of words to describe them.
It's all for you. He will tell you so himself.

CHORAGOS:

Is the man crazy?

EPOPS:

His sanity defies
definition.

CHORAGOS:

Really?

EPOPS:

Pure fox, subtle, deep.

CHORAGOS:

Then let him speak, let him speak!
These hints of yours have got me all a-twitter.

AGON

[*Order is now restored. As* EPOPS *takes command of the situation, the* CHORUS *forms itself at opposite sides of the* orchestra *to listen to the ensuing debate.*

EPOPS:

You there, and you,
carry these weapons in and hang them up
in the kitchen again, next to the tripod.
Fair fortune befall them!

[*Exeunt two Bird Servants with the pots, spits, and other utensils*

—And you, friend,
inform the Birds why I have summoned them
to this Assembly. Expound.

PISTHETAIROS:

No, by Apollo!
Not unless they promise me first
what Monk the Knifeman made that wife of his
promise *him*: no biting, no tickling, no unseemly
prodding in the—

EUELPIDES:

The arse, you would say?

PISTHETAIROS:

No;
I mean my eyes.

41

CHORAGOS:

Sir, you have our promise.

PISTHETAIROS:

Swear it.

CHORAGOS:

I swear it; but on condition that
this Comedy of ours wins First Prize
by unanimous vote of the judges and audience.

EPOPS:

NOW HEAR THIS:

Break ranks! Every private will pick up his arms
and go back to barracks. See your bulletin boards
for further announcements.

CHORUS:

Men were deceivers ever; and it may be,   [STROPHE
Friend, that the quality of our guilelessness
    Tempts you to gull us. Nevertheless,
        Nothing risked may be gain rejected when

Truth as a Stranger comes. If you have discerned
New forces in us, talents earthed over, dis-
    used instruments of old artifice:
        Speak out. Let age edify unfledged youth.

CHORAGOS:

You are at liberty to say whatever you like.

42

You have our promise:
We shall not be the first to break the truce.

PISTHETAIROS:

I thank you.

      —Gentlemen, you will find
much to chew on in the following message.
But first, with your permission—

                      [*To a* SERVANT

             Boy, bring me
a garland and a bowl of water to wash my hands.

EUELPIDES [*apart*]:

Do you see dinner coming?

PISTHETAIROS [*apart*]:

             No; I am trying to think
of something to tell them, some enormous concept
that will knock them silly.

           —Gentlemen: My heart
bleeds—bleeds, I say—when I reflect that you
who once were kings—

CHORAGOS:

          Kings? Kings of what?

PISTHETAIROS:

Why, kings of everything! Kings of myself, of this
poor friend of mine, yes, kings of Zeus the King!
Before Time was, you were: you antedate
Kronos, the Titans, Earth—

CHORAGOS:

Earth?

PISTHETAIROS:

Yes, by Heaven!

CHORAGOS:

That's something that I never knew before.

PISTHETAIROS:

Ignorance, acedia. There are authorities
for what I say: Aisôpos, to go no farther.
He tells us—don't you remember?—that the Lark
was the first Bird born in those chaotic times
before even Earth was thought of; and the Lark's
father died—have you forgotten?—, and because
there was no earth on Earth to bury him in,
the Lark finally laid him away in her head.

EUELPIDES:

Exactly. That's how Hyde Lark got its name.

PISTHETAIROS:

You see my point, I hope? If birds existed
before the Creation, before the gods themselves,
then you Birds must be heirs apparent: the royal power
belongs to you.

EUELPIDES:

Of course. At the same time,
they'd better keep their beaks in fighting trim:
Zeus won't give in to the first woodpecker.

44

PISTHETAIROS:

In those glorious days it was not the gods who ruled
over men, but the Birds. Let me cite you a few proofs.
Consider the Cock.
Long before any Dareioses or Megabazoses
the Cock was King of the Persians, and such a king
that ever since he's been called the Persian Bird.

EUELPIDES:

That's why, even now,
Cocks strut like the Shah; and of all birds living
only they have a right to the tiara.

PISTHETAIROS:

What power he had! Why, to this very day
when the Cock sings at dawn
everyone jumps out of bed and goes to work:
blacksmiths, potters, tanners, shoemakers,
grocers, masseurs, lyre-&-shield-manufacturers—
Some of them are hard at it before it's light.

EUELPIDES:

Some of them certainly are! That's how I lost
a perfectly good new Phrygian all-wool coat.
I'd been asked to a party to celebrate
naming somebody's baby. Well, when I got there
I had a couple of short ones, so I felt sleepy
and lay down for a minute; and—would you believe it?—
some damned cock began to crow, and I woke up
and thought it was morning, before the other guests

45

had even sat down to dinner! Well, I started out
on the Halimos road, but I'd hardly poked my nose
past the drive when, baff! somebody boffed me
with something blunt, and I went down for the count.
When I came to, my coat was somewhere else.

PISTHETAIROS:

At that same time the Kite reigned over the Greeks.

CHORAGOS:

The Greeks?

PISTHETAIROS:

                 The Greeks. That's when they learned
to prostrate themselves when the kites come back in the spring.

EUELPIDES:

I remember I prostrated myself one day
when I saw a Kite, or I tried to, but somehow
I fell on my back by mistake and my market money
went down my throat. That day I ate no more.

PISTHETAIROS:

Then there's the Cuckoo.
Once upon a time
in Egypt and in Phoinikia the Cuckoo
was king. As a matter of fact, when the Cuckoo
said 'Cuckoo!',
all the Phoinikians went out and mowed their fields.

EUELPIDES:

'Cuckoo! Back to the furrows, you foreskinless!'
as the proverb has it.

46

PISTHETAIROS:

Another thing: You will find
that whenever a man managed to become a king,
an Agamemnon, say, or a Menelaos,
he would always carry a bird on the end of his sceptre
to share the royal gifts.

EUELPIDES:

That explains something.
I used to go to the theatre; and whenever Priam
came on in the tragedies, he'd have a bird
on his sceptre, just as you say. I used to think
the bird was there to keep an eye on our friend
Lysikratês when the bribes were passed around.

PISTHETAIROS:

But the best proof is that Zeus, the current King,
wears an Eagle on his head as a sign of power.
His Daughter has an Owl; his son Apollo,
as a medical man, has a Hawk.

EUELPIDES:

That's perfectly true.
Why do you suppose those gods have those birds?

PISTHETAIROS:

Why? So that when the sacrificial roasts
are offered to the gods, the birds may taste them first.
And here's something else:
In the old days men never swore by the gods,
but always by birds.

EUELPIDES:

Lampôn still does today.

He always says 'Holy Kites!' when he makes a mistake.

PISTHETAIROS:

You understand, then, that years and years ago
you were great, even holy, in the minds of men.

But now? Now you are rejects, fools,
worse than slaves, stoned
in the streets by arrogant men, hunted
down even in your sanctuaries
by trappers with nets, springes, limed
twigs, cages, decoy-
boxes;

caught, sold
wholesale, goosed, prodded
by fat fingers, denied
even the grace of wholesome frying,
but served up sleazily, choked
with cheese, smeared with oil,
sprayed with vinegar, doused
as though you were dead meat, too gamy,
in rivers of sweet slab sauce.

CHORUS: [ANTISTROPHE

Tears, and no idle tears, Stranger, distress us
Hearing your plain account of calamity.

48

    Clearly our primeval dignity
        Has lapsed in the long sliding of the years.

   You, by a happy chance or some divine in-
   fluence sent to guide us, have indicated
      Future recovery, joy ahead.
          Ourselves, our wives, our chicks depend on you.

CHORAGOS:

  What can we do? Instruct us, since you say
  you have a plan. Life's no life for us
  till we win back the power that we have lost.

PISTHETAIROS:

  My plan is a great City for All Birds,
  a single City, with the surrounding air
  and all the space between encircled by
  massive brick walls like those at Babylon.

EUELPIDES:

  Bring on your Giants! What a mighty fortress!

PISTHETAIROS:

  Once the wall's built, you must send an embassy
  to Zeus and lay your grievances before him.
  If he denies them, if he temporizes,
  then you should declare a Holy War
  against the whole of Olympos: no more free passage
  for divinities in an obvious state of erection
  on their way through your land to flirt with their Alopês,

49

their Sémelês, their Alkmenês! No; once across the border,
each strutting member must be stamped and sealed.
That should give them something to think about!

As for Mankind,
you must send another bird to them, a herald
to announce that from now on, since the Birds are kings,
the first sacrifices must be made to them,
and then (if convenient) to the Olympian gods.
But even in sacrifices to the gods
an appropriate Bird must be adored as well:
thus, Aphroditê and a Phalarope; Poseidôn
and a Duck; Heraklês and a Cormorant;
or, if the victim is offered up to King Zeus,
let the Wren, the Wren, the king of all birds, receive
the flesh of the Balled Gnat.

EUELPIDES:

What price gnat-flesh?
Let the Good Gosh bounce thunderballs in the sky!

CHORAGOS:

What if men refuse to treat us as gods?
What if they say, 'Them? Jackdaws, that's all,
'flying around up there with their silly wings'?

PISTHETAIROS:

I can't believe you are serious. Why, good Lord!
Hermês has wings, and he flies; yes, and Nikê,
she has wings; and Erôs—all sorts of gods
fly, don't they? Why, even Iris,

50

the one that Homer refers to as 'Trembling Dove'—
Iris has wings, Iris flies.

EUELPIDES:

Speaking of wings,
what if Zeus drops one of his wingèd bolts on us?

CHORAGOS:

But what if Mankind is so unregenerate
that only the regulars of the Olympos clique
are recognized?

PISTHETAIROS:

We'll draft a regiment
of Sparrows and march them off to steal the seeds
in the new-planted fields. Deméter can set up
a Farm Program to fend off starvation.

EUELPIDES:

Deméter will also find a thousand ways
to get around any program that she sets up.

PISTHETAIROS:

If the Sparrows fail, we'll send some Elite Crows
to the grazing lands and have them bite out the eyes
of herdsmen and herds. Let Apollo cure them:
he's a doctor, he gets paid.

EUELPIDES:

Let me know in advance:
I'll want to sell my yoke of oxen first.

PISTHETAIROS:

But if they sense the indwelling divinity

51

of the Birds, as they should, knowing that you are God,
and Life, and Earth, and Kronos, and Poseidôn—
then everything will end as they would have it.

CHORAGOS:

Everything? What do you mean?

PISTHETAIROS:

                         For example,
locusts will not touch their budding vines:
the Hawks and Owls will see to that. Then, too,
a single platoon of indoctrinated Redwings
will be assigned to keep the gall-flies and emmets
from chewing up fig-shoots.

CHORAGOS:

                        But how shall we manage
money? Men seem to set great store by money.

PISTHETAIROS:

The Auspice birds will show them where rich mines
lie in the earth. The Augurs, too, will learn
the secret of quick returns. Shipwrecks will end—

CHORAGOS:

How so?

PISTHETAIROS:

              They'll consult the Birds before each voyage:
'Is it safe to sail?' 'Not today; a storm's blowing up.'

EUELPIDES:

I'll invest in a boat. Yo-ho for the briny deep!

52

PISTHETAIROS:

Then, of course, there are those buried pots
of treasure. The Birds know. Haven't you heard
'A little bird told me where to look for it'?

EUELPIDES:

I'll sell my boat. Me for the buried pots!

CHORAGOS:

But what about health? That's the gift of the gods.

PISTHETAIROS:

When business is good, health takes care of itself.

EUELPIDES:

I never heard of a bankrupt whose health was good.

CHORAGOS:

How will they ever live to reach old age?
Surely that's an Olympian dispensation.
Or must they die in the cradle?

PISTHETAIROS:

                          Not at all.
The Birds will add three centuries to their lives.

CHORAGOS:

Where will they get three centuries?

PISTHETAIROS:

                          From themselves.
The poet says:
'One crow caws down five generations of man'.

EUELPIDES:

Almost thou persuadest me to be a bird.

53

PISTHETAIROS:

Why not be birds? They demand no marble temples
intricate with golden doors; their shrines
are the ilex, the sparkling shrubs. Their highest gods
live in the sanctuary of olive trees.
We need no Delphoi or Ammon for this worship,
but at home, on our own ground,
in peace among our own familiar flowers,
we can raise hands full of grain to them in prayer,
invoking their dear aid:
and when our words fly up, they will be answered
in blessings that fall upon the scattered grain.

CHORAGOS:

Dearest of old men, you have won me utterly
to your cause. From this hour your words are my words.

CHORUS:

My mind applauds.
Swear faith to me,
And I will swear
Death to the gods.
The fight is fair:
Sing Victory.

CHORAGOS:

We are ready to do whatever must be done.
The plans and stratagems we leave to you.

54

EPOPS:

    Action, quick action. By God, this is no time
for taking naps or dawdling like Nikias!
But first, gentlemen,
this is my nest, a poor thing of twigs and straw,
but my own. Will you permit me to entertain you
inside? And will you tell me who you are?

PISTHETAIROS:

    Of course. Pisthetairos is the name. That one's
Euelpidês; comes from Kriôa.

EPOPS:

                    Very happy
to meet you both.

PISTHETAIROS:

           Not at all.

EPOPS:

                  Will you please step in?

PISTHETAIROS:

    After you.

EPOPS:

        Right this way.

PISTHETAIROS:

             There, I almost forgot!
Tell me, how can a couple of men like us
live with birds? You can fly. We don't know how.

EPOPS:

    I see.

PISTHETAIROS:

And speaking of Aisôpos again,
he has a fable about a fox and an eagle.
The fox lost.

EPOPS:

Really, it's no problem at all.
There's a useful little herb. You nibble it
and, presto!—you sprout wings.

PISTHETAIROS:

That's fair enough.
—Here, Xanthias, Manodôros: pick up the baggage.

CHORAGOS:

Hi! Epops! Before you go—

EPOPS:

What's the matter?

CHORAGOS:

You'll invite our venerable guests to dine, of course;
but the Nightingale,
the Muses' love, sweet cataract of song—
will you send her out and let us play with her?

PISTHETAIROS:

A sound idea, by God, and I second it.
Ask the delightful bird to step this way.

EUELPIDES:

Yes, just for a minute. You can't imagine how long
we've longed, my friend and I, for a nightingale.

56

EPOPS:

You are too kind.

—Proknê, Proknê,

come here and show yourself to our noble guests.

[*Enter the* Nightingale: *a flute-girl, nude except for her mask and wings*

PISTHETAIROS:

God of our fathers, what a heavenly little bird!
So soft, so white—
How I should like to get between those thighs!

EUELPIDES:

The gold, all the gold, like a bride on her wedding day!
I can't help it; I am obliged to kiss this young woman.

PISTHETAIROS:

Stupid, don't you see the little spikes on her beak?
You'll get hurt.

EUELPIDES:

No, I shan't. It's like opening an egg.
Tap her on the head, the shell falls away,
and there's my kiss.

EPOPS [*indicating the door*]:

Gentlemen.

PISTHETAIROS:

Let's go in.

[*Exeunt*

57

PARÁBASIS I

[*In the* orchestra *the* CHORUS *turns to face the audience; the* Nightingale *accompanies the lyric passages
on her flute.*

CHORUS [*a solo voice*]:

Tawnythroat, Partner   [KOMMATION
In song, dark
Muse, dearest of Birds:
Come, let the curving long
Line of your fluting
Fall, sparkling
Undersong to our words.

CHORAGOS: [PARABASIS

Come now, let us consider the generations of Man,
Compound of dust and clay, strengthless,
Tentative, passing away as leaves in autumn
Pass, shadows wingless, forlorn
Phantoms deathbound, a dream. Let Men turn
To the Birds, aerial philosophers of
Forever, safe from age, from change, from death.
Let them be humble and learn from us
The truth of Being, the essential germ,
The Bird, first Cause of Gods and Rivers,
Of Erebos, and of the great Void of Chaos.

Here is the absolute Theogony:
Professor Pródikos can lecture somewhere else.

61

CHAOS and NIGHT: that was the start of it,
And black Erebos, and the long nothing of Tártaros;
No Earth as yet, no Air, no Heaven. There,
In the untried lap of Erebos, sombre Night
Laid a wind-egg, whence, with the circling year,
Erôs was hatched, golden Erôs, wínd-swíft
Love, the world's longing. His was the sleight
Joined Night and wingèd Chaos in that first
Tartarean marriage and brought the race of Birds
To the shores of light. It was Erôs
Created the line of Gods also, mixing
The urgent elements in adorable ways
To make the Sky and Sea and Earth and all
The Blessèd Ones.

        So it appears that we
Are móre ancient than these same Blessèd Ones,
Older in the line of Love. What I say is clear
In a thousand proofs:

        We are wing'd, and so is Love.
Love is our art: how many a handsome boy
Has armed his heart with scorn, only to yield
His proud thighs to the persuasion of the Birds,
Won by a gift of quail, or geese, or cocks!

And birds are good to men in numberless ways.
We lead in the seasons. The clanging Crane
Flies towards Libya, and the sowing begins;

She it is who tells the mariner
When it is time to take his winter sleep,
The unshipped rudder hanging against the wall.
This same Crane
Inspires our friend Orestês of the Alleys
To knit himself a shirt against the cold,
Thus winning the gratitude of citizens waylaid
Who otherwise would shiver in nudity.
Later, the Kite brings back the brilliant Spring
And you barber your sheep; and then the summer Swallow
Suggests bargains of thin dress at the shops.

We are Ammon, Delphoi, Dodôna, Phoibos Apollo.
Are you not always taking the advice of birds
In matters of business, of marriage, of daily life?
You see Bird in everything: your rumours are what
A small Bird told you; your sneeze is a Bird, your chance
Hello in the street's a Bird; a stranger encountered;
An ass on the road: all Birds, all signs of Birds.
Are we not right to call ourselves your Apollos?

Therefore confess us gods, for so   [MAKRON
We are, to you; and you shall have
Feathery Muses to foretell
The winter wind, the summer breeze.
We will not perch like Zeus, at ease
In some remote cloud-citadel,

63

But live with you and with your sons,
Your sons' sons, and their sons as well,
Bringing you gifts of youth and peace,
Love, laughter, wealth, new dances, brave
Festivals, more than the human tongue
Can tell, more than the heart can know.
This is our pledge, this is our song.

CHORUS:

Woodland Muse

[ODE

tiotiotínx tiotínx

Lucency

Darting voice

Valley

Wanderer, circling flight

tiotínx tiotiotínx

on the bright hills:

My singing

Spills

duskiness into the light

For Pan

and thou hearest

For

The Great Mother, Mountaindweller,

tótotototótotototínx

and thou

hearest

In air

    on the heights

        fields

     where Phrynichos

  Tastes the ambrosial finality

     tiotínx

        of song.

CHORAGOS: [EPIRRHEMA

If any gentleman in the audience is interested
In a pleasant life, he should get in touch with us.
We practise what your laws forbid: You would like to beat
Your father? Good. According to your code
It's an off-colour pastime and, moreover, illegal.
All right; but if you were one of us Birds,
You'd just walk up to the old man, tap him
On the snout, and say: 'Put 'em up, if you want to fight!'
Or say you're on the lam, branded and all that: here,
We'd refer to you as a Mottled Francolin, and forget you.
You're a sub-asiatic type like Spíntharos?
Here you'd be a Migrant Finch, Philêmon species.
Even a creeping calamity like Exekestidês
Can hatch ancestors up here and become respectable.
Why, if Peisias' son himself
Should take after the old man and cohabit
With subversives by the dozens, we'd only say
'What a clever bird he is, always drumming up trade!'

CHORUS:

So the wild Swans   [ANTODE
tiotiotinx tiotinx
calling
Above the roar
Of their great wings,
cry
tiotinx tiotiotinx
'Apollo!'
on the Hebros
Shore:
The company
Of spotted wood-beasts fly
for dread,
The sea
hearing
tótototótototinx
falls
hearing
and is still:
Olympos
is hushed
The Graces
shriek back against
The liquid instancy
tiotinx
of song.

66

CHORAGOS: [ANTEPIRRHEMA

There is nothing more practical or more enjoyable
Than a pair of wings. Suppose you go to the theatre
And find it's some Tragedy or other: well, of course
You're bored, and hungry, so off you fly home,
Take care of your belly, and get back for the last act.
Or say you develop a sudden case of the runs.
Do you sit there and spoil your suit? No. You simply
Zoom up into the air, do your job, fart twice,
Catch your breath, and coast back to your seat again.
Or maybe you're an Adulterer, of all things, and there's
Your girl's husband in the front row gawking at the Chorus.
A flap of the wings, and you're off you know where; and when
You've laid the lady—a flap of the wings, and you're back.
Wings? There's nothing like them!
Look at Dieitrephês, if you want a good example:
Those wicker wing baskets he manufactures got him
A captaincy, then a colonelcy, and now, rags to riches,
He's a full-fledged Horsecock in a yellow uniform!

67

SCENE

[*Re-enter* PISTHETAIROS *and* EUELPIDES. *Both are now absurdly feathered, winged, and beaked.*

PISTHETAIROS:

So far, so good.

EUELPIDES:

By God, it's the funniest thing
I ever saw in my life!

PISTHETAIROS:

What is?

EUELPIDES:

You,
with those pinfeathers. Know what you look like?

PISTHETAIROS:

You look like a cut-rate reproduction
of an unsuccessful sketch of a goose.

EUELPIDES:

Do I?
You look like a blackbird tonsured in the dark.

PISTHETAIROS:

These similes are futile. Remember the poem:
'I shot an arrow into the air . . .'

CHORAGOS:

Next business?

PISTHETAIROS:

First we must find

a name for our City, a glorious name;
and then we must sacrifice to the gods.

EUELPIDES:

You said it.

CHORAGOS:

Let's get busy. What shall we call this City of ours?

PISTHETAIROS:

Shall we go in for a touch of Lakonian *je ne sais quoi*
and name it New Sparta?

EUELPIDES:

I want no part of Sparta.
Gosh, I wouldn't tie a name like that
to a flop-house bunk!

PISTHETAIROS:

Well, have you any ideas?

EUELPIDES:

Somewhere, what with all these clouds and all this air,
there must be a rare name, somewhere . . .

PISTHETAIROS:

How do you like
'Cloudcuckooland'?

CHORAGOS:

That's it! That's it!
What a name, what a jewel of a name you've thought of!

EUELPIDES:

Cloudcuckooland. Isn't that the place
where Aischenês and Theogenês rent castles?

72

PISTHETAIROS:

Yes; and it's where the Giants met the Gods
and got themselves bluffed off the battlefield.

CHORAGOS:

Cloudcuckooland's a city with a future!
What god or goddess shall we choose for Patron?

EUELPIDES:

Why not Athenê?

PISTHETAIROS:

In a City with a Future,
'what boots a mailèd warrior goddess in arms',
since Kleisthenês tends to the weaving?

CHORAGOS:

But the Akropolis?
Who will guard the Pelargic Wall?

PISTHETAIROS:

A bird.

CHORAGOS:

One of us? What kind?

PISTHETAIROS:

Something Persian, I should say,
something with a reputation for ferocity.
An Arês-chicken, maybe?

EUELPIDES:

Hail, Arês, Master Cluck!
He's used to uncomfortable roosts, at any rate.

PISTHETAIROS:

But now,

off you go into the air! See what the builders
are up to. Make sure they have enough stones.
Get plenty of tubs. Make the mortar yourself. (Better
strip first.) Carry the hods up—

EUELPIDES:

And fall off the ladder.

PISTHETAIROS:

Bank the fires. Post sentries in the right places.
Make the round of the guards at night—

EUELPIDES:

And take a snooze.

PISTHETAIROS:

Send out two heralds, one to the gods above,
one to mankind below.
When you have done this, report back here to me.

EUELPIDES:

And here you'll be on your back! I wish to God
you'd do some of the work.

PISTHETAIROS:

Friend, that's not like you.
We all depend on you to get things done.
I shall be busy too:

[*Exit* EUELPIDES

I must arrange for the dedication service
and collar a priest to recite the liturgy.
Boy!—You, boy!—Bring me the basket and the lavabo.

74

CHORUS:

Inevitably right! My mind   [STROPHE
   Melts in your mind's embrace.
High rituals of any kind
   Are proper in this place.
Here let our piety devote
To the blest gods one skinny goat.

So may they look down from above
   Upon our sacred feast,
Accept our sparsely offered love,
   And overlook the rest.
Sing one, sing all! Sing deaf, sing mute!
Chairis, assist us with your flute.

PISTHETAIROS [*to the* Fluteplayer]:

You, there, stop that futile tooting!
What a man! I swear by my God, I've seen
strange sights in my life, but this is the first
crow I ever saw with a leather beak-rest.

[*Enter a* PRIEST

Holiness, get busy. Sacrifice to the gods.

PRIEST:

I would fain do so.

       —Where is my acolyte?

75

LET US PRAY:

TO HESTIA NESTIARCH, TO THE HIGH HAWK
OF THE HALL, TO ALL OLYMPIAN BIRDS AND
BIRDETTES—

PISTHETAIROS:

Hail Storkissimo! Hail, Super of Sounion!

PRIEST:

—TO THE PYTHODELIAN SWAN, TO LETO CORN-
CRAKE, TO ARTEMIS SISKIN—

PISTHETAIROS:

That's a pretty association of ideas!

PRIEST:

—TO SABAZIOS THE PHRYGILLATOR, TO THE
GREAT OSTRICH MOTHER OF GODS AND MEN—

PISTHETAIROS:

Lady Kybelê, Ostrichess, Mother of Kleokritos!

PRIEST:

THAT THEY MAY VOUCHSAFE HEALTH AND
LENGTH OF DAYS TO ALL CLOUDCUCKOO-
LANDERS, and also to the Chians—

PISTHETAIROS:

My heart leaps up when someone mentions the Chians!

PRIEST:

AND TO ALL HERO BIRDS AND BIRDSONS OF HE-
ROES: MORE ESPECIALLY TO THE PORPHYRION,
THE WRY PECKER, THE PELICAN, THE PYRO-
PHLEX, THE RUDDY GUINEA, THE PEACOCK,

76

THE MAJOR OUSEL, THE TEAL, THE BANDED
BITTERN, THE HERON, THE DISTELFINK, THE
BALMY PETREL, THE PIPIT, THE GOATGREEN
TITMOUSE, THE—

PISTHETAIROS:

Birds, birds, birds! Enough! Why, what a man
you are, to summon all those vultures and sea-eagles
to our Eucharist! Can't you see that a single hawk
could take our entire victim at one gulp?
Go away, and take your portable altar with you.

[*Exit* PRIEST

I'll finish the service myself.

CHORUS:

      If that is so, it seems that I   [ANTISTROPHE
        Must tune my voice again
    In sacramental hymnody
      Of even deeper strain:
    O Gods, and thou our Patron's God,
    Exact no more from us than laud.

    Behold our sacrificial beast,
      Sick bones and stringy hair:
    If you partake of the thin feast,
      How shall we laymen fare?
    Reject our poor oblation, then,
    And feed your worshipers. Amen.

77

PISTHETAIROS:

Let us propitiate the Feathery Gods.

[*Enter a* POET, *singing*

POET:

Cloudcuckooland, my happy home,
Sung by the Muses Nine—

PISTHETAIROS:

How did this one get in?

—Who are you?

POET:

Who am I? A honeythroated bard,
a 'willing slave of the Muse', as Homer puts it.

PISTHETAIROS:

A slave? With that haircut?

POET:

You misunderstand.

I am a poet. All we poets are
'willing slaves of the Muse', as Homer puts it.

PISTHETAIROS:

That cloak of yours has seen service, willing or not.
Speak, O Bard: What catastrophe brings you here?

POET:

In honour of Cloudcuckooland, that great City,
I have composed the following lyric items:
    a] a batch of cyclic verses
    b] a few simple virginations
    c] some odes in the manner of Simonidês.

78

PISTHETAIROS:

God forbid. When did you start writing them?

POET:

Long have I meditated on this City, long.

PISTHETAIROS:

Impossible. Why, only a minute ago

I was dedicating the place, giving it a name!

POET:

Ah, swift is the speech of the Muses,

Yea, swifter than swivelling steeds!

Mark me, man:

Thou Author of Aitna, Father,

At whose dire doom do foregather

All the high hierarchs—

Och! wad

Thy nod

Some giftie gi'e me:

I don't care what, just a token of your regard.

PISTHETAIROS:

He'll be around all day if we don't pay him off.

Here, you in the new overcoat:

take it off and give it to this lyric has-been.

—Put it on. You look as though you were catching cold.

POET:

Thy, Sir, high gratuity

Compels gratitudinity.

79

Brace yourself. I will now address you
in the vein of Pindar.

PISTHETAIROS:

It's a vein I can do without.

POET:

Ill fares the man amid the Skythian spears,
Beset by Nomads, who no 'pparel wears.
Nil is his number, nameless is his name,
Who hath no garment to refúge his shame.
Do you get me?

PISTHETAIROS:

I get the idea that you want some underwear.
—Take that off too, man, and let him have it.
He's a poet, after all.

—There you are. Get out!

POET:

Out, out, poor poet!
Sing, O Muse in gold enthroned,
This chilly City!
Naked in many a snowbank have I moaned,
Which seems a pity.
But still I'll chant, where'er I roam,
Cloudcuckooland my happy home.
Alalaí!

[*Exit* POET

80

[952-965]

PISTHETAIROS:

God, what a nuisance! I hope I never meet
another one like that. How did he hear so soon
about our City? Well . . .

—You, there:
Go around again with the holy water.

[*Enter a* TRAVELLING PROPHET

DEARLY BELOVED: WE GATHER TOGETHER IN—
PROPHET:

Silence!

Begin not the sacrifice of the goat!
PISTHETAIROS:

Who says so?
PROPHET:

I; an Expounder of Oracles.
PISTHETAIROS:

Expounders be damned!
PROPHET:

Tut. We mustn't blaspheme.
I come to reveal an oracle of Bakis
that bears directly on Cloudcuckooland.
PISTHETAIROS:

In God's name, why did you wait to reveal it
until I'd gone and founded Cloudcuckooland?
PROPHET:

God moves in a mysterious way.

81

PISTHETAIROS:

He does.

Well, since you're here, let's have your revelation.

PROPHET:

WHAT TIME WOLVES AND WHITE CROWS
CONFECT BUNGALOWS
'TWIXT SIKYON AND KORINTH—

PISTHETAIROS:

It's a lie! I never had any dealings with Korinth.

PROPHET:

That is Bakis' way of referring to the Air.

Now listen:

TO PANDORA THIS DAY
A WHITE RAM THOU MUST SLAY,
AND TO WHOSO DIVINES ME THOU SHALT
NOT REFUSE
A WARM WINTER SUIT AND A PAIR OF NEW
SHOES.

PISTHETAIROS:

Does it say shoes?

PROPHET:

Look in the book.

PLUS A GENEROUS CUP,
PLUS A SLICE OFF THE TOP—

PISTHETAIROS:

A slice off the top, hey?

82

PROPHET:

Look in the book.

AND IF, GODLY INFANT, THOU DOST AS I SAY,
A HEAV'N-KISSING EAGLE SHALT THOU BE
    TODAY,
NOT SO MUCH AS A TITTYMOUSE IF THOU
    SAY'ST NAY.

PISTHETAIROS:

Is that there too?

PROPHET:

Look in the book.

PISTHETAIROS:

Strange. It's so unlike the oracle
I took down from Apollo's dictation.

PROPHET:

What was that one?

PISTHETAIROS:

BUT IF BY ILL HAP A CHEAP ORACLE-MONGER
DISTURBETH THE SERVICE WITH LIES BORN OF
    HUNGER,
THOU SHALT BASH IN HIS RIBS—

PROPHET:

I don't believe it says that.

PISTHETAIROS:

Look in the book.

AS FOR HEAV'N-KISSING EAGLES AND ARSE-
    KISSING SEERS,

83

TO HELL WITH THEM ALL. END OF MESSAGE.
[LOUD CHEERS]

PROPHET:

Is that there too?

PISTHETAIROS:

Look in the book.

[*Suddenly losing patience*

Damn you, get out of here!

[*Strikes him with his staff*

PROPHET:

Ouch! I'll go! Ouch!

[*Exit* PROPHET

PISTHETAIROS [*calling after him*]:

Peddle your damned oracles somewhere else!

[*Enter* METON, *wearing a saffron gown embroidered with geometrical figures*

METON:

My aim in coming here—

PISTHETAIROS:

Another headache!
What's your project? And, above all,
why that absurd costume?

84

METON:

I have come
to subdivide the air into square acres.

PISTHETAIROS:

May I ask who you are?

METON:

You may. My name is Metôn.
The word's a commonplace in Greece and Kolonos.

PISTHETAIROS:

What's that you've got with you?

METON:

An aerial straight-edge.
Observe:
The conformation of the air, considered as
a total entity, is that of a conical damper.
Very well. At the apex of this cone we apply
the ruler, bracketing in the dividers to allow
for the congruent curve. Q.E.D.

PISTHETAIROS:

Q.E.D.?

METON:

We calculate the declination by cathexis
according to the sine. Thus we square the circle.
In the centre we postulate a forum, the focus
of convergent streets that, stelliform,
subtend the radii extended from this point.
Q.E.D.

PISTHETAIROS:

Q.E.D.! The man's a Thalês!
Metôn.

METON:

Yes?

PISTHETAIROS:

I admire you. I really do.
Take my advice and subdivide somewhere else.

METON:

Why? Is it dangerous here?

PISTHETAIROS:

Yes, here and in Sparta.
You know how they're treating aliens these days:
nasty demonstrations in the streets.

METON:

You apprehend
seditious manifestations in Cloudcuckooland?

PISTHETAIROS:

God forbid.

METON:

Then what?

PISTHETAIROS:

Well, we've passed a law
that charlatans shall be whipped in the public square.

METON:

Oh. Then I'd better be going.

PISTHETAIROS:

You're almost too late.
Here's a sample, God help you!

[*Knocks him down*

METON:

My head! My head!

PISTHETAIROS:

I warned you. On your way, and be quick about it!

[*Exit* METON; *enter an* INSPECTOR, *elegant in full uniform, carrying two urns for balloting*

INSPECTOR:

Summon the Consuls.

PISTHETAIROS:

Who's this Sardanápalos?

INSPECTOR:

My good man, I am a legally designated
Inspector, empowered to investigate
the civic status of Cloudcuckooland.

PISTHETAIROS:

Your warrant?

INSPECTOR:

This illegible document
endorsed by Teleas.

PISTHETAIROS:

My dear Inspector,

it seems a pity to waste your valuable time.

Suppose you collect your pay and go right home?

INSPECTOR:

A first-rate idea! As a matter of fact,

I ought not to have left Athens at all.

There are certain sensitive foreign affairs—you know?—

that Pharnakês leaves to me.

PISTHETAIROS:

Is that so?

Here's your pay.

[*Slaps his face*

INSPECTOR:

Sir, I demand the meaning of this.

PISTHETAIROS:

It's a sensitive foreign affair.

INSPECTOR:

I make formal protest

that you have assaulted and battered an Inspector.

PISTHETAIROS:

Take your voting-jugs and get out of my sight!

It's an outrage:

Inspectors before there's a City to inspect!

[*The* INSPECTOR *withdraws, but hides behind one of the Acolytes; enter a* DECREE-VENDOR, *who begins to read from a scroll:*

88

DECREE-VENDOR:

'AND IF ANY CLOUDCUCKOOLANDER WHATSO-
EVER SHALL CAUSE INJURY OR DISTRESS TO
ANY ATHENIAN CITIZEN WHATSOEVER—'

PISTHETAIROS:

Another one! A walking law-book this time.

DECREE-VENDOR:

Your Honour, I am a dealer in the latest decrees.
Satisfaction guaranteed.

PISTHETAIROS:

As for example?

DECREE-VENDOR:

'VOTED: THAT FROM THE DATE HEREINUNDER
SUBSCRIBED ALL WEIGHTS MEASURES AND
STATUTES WHATSOEVER OF CLOUDCUCKOO-
LAND SHALL BE IDENTICAL WITH THE SAME
OBTAINING IN OLOPHYXOS.'

PISTHETAIROS:

That ought to fix us.

—Look here, you!

DECREE-VENDOR:

What's the matter with you? Something you ate?

PISTHETAIROS:

Go back where you came from with your silly laws,
or you'll get some rough and ready legislation.

[*Strikes him; exit* DECREE-VENDOR *hurriedly; the* IN-
SPECTOR *reappears.*

INSPECTOR:

  I charge Pisthetairos with felonious assault,
  returnable April Session.

PISTHETAIROS:

                 How did *you* get back?

                [*The* DECREE-VENDOR *re-enters.*

DECREE-VENDOR:

  'AND IF ANY MAN SHALL SCUTTLE A MAGIS-
  TRATE AFTER THE NAME OF SAME HAS BEEN
  POSTED ON THE PILLAR IN ACCORDANCE WITH
  THE LAW—'

PISTHETAIROS:

  Holy God! You too?

             [*Drives him away with blows*

INSPECTOR:

  I'll have your license! This will cost you a cool thousand!

PISTHETAIROS:

  I'll smash those jugs of yours in a thousand pieces!

INSPECTOR:

  Do you remember the evening you polluted the pillar?

PISTHETAIROS:

  Go pollute yourself!

            —Grab him! That's it!

[INSPECTOR *escapes.*

Let's hope that's the end of him.

— Gentlemen:
If we're going to sacrifice our goat at all,
I'm afraid we'll have to do the job inside.

[*Exeunt; manet* CHORUS

PARÁBASIS II

[*The* CHORUS *again addresses itself to the audience:*

CHORUS:

We are Lords of Earth and of all upon it,⠀⠀⠀⠀[ODE
Marking all, all-knowing, in tireless session
Guiding, weighing, judging the varied drama.
⠀⠀Come and adore us!

Guardians of young fruit in the open orchards,
Our swift beaks transfix the insect marauder,
And he falls, struck down by the feath'ry ictus
⠀⠀Whirring from heaven.

CHORAGOS:⠀⠀⠀⠀⠀⠀⠀⠀⠀⠀⠀⠀⠀⠀⠀⠀[EPIRRHEMA

You see CRIMINAL WANTED notices everywhere:
'Whoever kills Diágoras the Mêlian,'
So much reward; 'Whoever kills
'A dead tyrant or so,' still more
Reward. Well, then, I proclaim:
'Whoever kills Philókratês the Birdseller,
'One talent, cash; whoever brings him in
'Alive, four talents'—twice as much
As for poor old Diágoras. This Philókratês
Hangs bullfinches on hooks in his shop
And sells them at cut rates; he inflates thrushes
With air pumps and exposes their abused puffy
Bodies for sale; he mutilates blackbirds; he

Stuffs live pigeons into nets and makes them
Act as decoys. That's Philókratês for you!

—And

If any members of this audience
Maintain a bird in a gilded cage at home,
We beg you let it go. Refuse, and you'll see
How quickly the Birds will make decoys of you!

CHORUS:

Joy of birds! In summer the long thick sunlight   [ANTODE
When the locust drones in the trance of noontime:
Mad with sun we shout, and the forest dances
       Heavy with music.

Wintertime is sun on the tropic headlands
Where the Nymphs play counterpoint to our singing;
Spring is myrtle, pang of the pink sweet prickling
       Buds of the Graces.

CHORAGOS:

Now for a word or two, Judges, about   [ANTEPIRRHEMA
This Competition. If you give us the Prize,
We'll pay you better for it than Prince Paris
Was paid by the Goddess. First of all,
The Owls of Laureion will never desert you:
They'll be everywhere in your houses, nesting
In your purses, maniacally producing
Miniature Owls. Judges are fond of Owls.

96

More than that, we'll add new wings
To your houses: you'll dream that you dwell
In marble halls, and you'll be right.

If your jobs

Are slow pay, if your fingers begin to itch,
We'll send you a little confidential Hawk
To perch on your wrist. For state dinners you can have
The loan of a bird-crop to solve capacity problems.
But if we lose the Prize,
Take portable canopies with you on your strolls,
Or your new white robes will suffer
Avine criticism dropping from the skies.

SCENE

[*Re-enter* PISTHETAIROS *with his attendants*

PISTHETAIROS:

The omens are favourable, I'm glad to say.
Strange that we've had no news
about the wall.

    —But here comes a messenger now,
puffing like an Olympic sprinter.

[*Enter* FIRST MESSENGER, *wildly*

MESSENGER:

Where is he? Where is he? Where is he?

PISTHETAIROS:

    Where is who?

MESSENGER:

The Chief. Pisthetairos.

PISTHETAIROS:

    Here.

MESSENGER:

    Great news! Great news!
Your Wall is finished!

PISTHETAIROS:

    That *is* great news.

MESSENGER:

    Oh how
shall I describe the splendour of that Wall,
the apocalyptic hugeness? Take two chariots,

hitch four fat Wooden Horses to each one,
let Theogenês and old Proxenidês
of Belchertown meet head-on—, they'd pass each other
without a scratch. It's that big.

PISTHETAIROS:

Holy Heraklês!

MESSENGER:

And tall? Look, I measured it myself:
it stands six hundred feet!

PISTHETAIROS:

Merciful Poseidon!
What workmen could build a wall as high as that?

MESSENGER:

Birds, only birds. Not a single Egyptian
hodcarrier or stonemason or carpenter
in the gang; birds did it all, and my eyes
are popping yet.

Imagine thirty thousand Cranes
from Libya, each one with a belly full of stones
for the Rails to shape up with their beaks; ten
thousand Storks, at least,
all of them making bricks with clay and water
flown up by Curlews from the earth below.

PISTHETAIROS:

Mortar?

MESSENGER:

Herons with hods.

102

PISTHETAIROS:

How did they manage it?

MESSENGER:

That was a triumph of technology!
The Geese shovelled it up with their big feet.

PISTHETAIROS:

Ah feet, to what use can ye not be put!

MESSENGER:

Why, good Lord! There were Ducks to set the bricks,
and flights of little apprentice Swallows
with trowel tails for the mortar in their bills.

PISTHETAIROS:

Who wants hired labour after this?
—But the joists and beams?

MESSENGER:

All handled by birds.
When the Woodpeckers went to work on those portals
it sounded like a shipyard!

—So there's your Wall,
complete with gates and locks, watchfires burning,
patrols circling, the guard changed every hour.

But I must wash off this long trek of mine.
You'll know what to do next.

[*Exit* FIRST MESSENGER

CHORAGOS:

Surprises you, hey? That quick job on your Wall?

PISTHETAIROS:

Surprises me? Why, it's a lie come true!
But here's another non-stop messenger,
and this one looks like trouble.

[*Enter* SECOND MESSENGER: *tragic manner*

MESSENGER:

Alas! Alas! Alas!

PISTHETAIROS:

What's the matter with *you?*

MESSENGER:

Confusion now hath made his masterpiece!
One of the gods, I do not know his name,
has invaded our air and slipped through the gate
right under the beaks of the Jackdaws on day duty.

PISTHETAIROS:

Murther and treason!

—What god did you say?

MESSENGER:

Identity not established. But he has wings,
we know that.

PISTHETAIROS:

Alert the Air Cadets!

MESSENGER:

Cadets! We've alerted everything we have.

104

Ten thousand mounted Arrowhawks,
to say nothing of claw-to-claw raiders
of every calibre: Kestrels, Buzzards,
Kites, Vultures, Nighthawks, Eagles—
every mortal inch of air
they've ploughed up with their wings, looking for that god.
He won't get away,
he's somewhere around here; I feel it in my feathers.

PISTHETAIROS:

Slings and arrows, slings and arrows! All of you,
here: get shooting, quick! Give me my bow!

CHORUS:

War to the end,   [STROPHE

Inexpressible war,

God against Bird!

Arm to defend

Our fathers' Air!

Olympos' host

Must not get past

Our border guard!

CHORAGOS:

Each one of you keep watch on every side.
I hear, or seem to hear, an ominous clack
of wings, as though some Deity were descending.

105

[*The goddess* IRIS *appears from above, suspended in the* machina; *she has broad static wings and wears a large rainbow around her head and shoulders.*

PISTHETAIROS:

Heave to! Let go halyards! Lower the flaps! Easy all!

[*The* machina *stops with a violent jerk.*

Who are you? Where are you bound? What's your home port?

IRIS [*tragic tone*]:

I come to you from the Olympian gods.

PISTHETAIROS:

Your name? Are you sea-going, or a flying
hat-rack?

IRIS:

Fleet Iris am I.

PISTHETAIROS:

Deep sea or
inland waters?

IRIS:

What *are* you talking about?

PISTHETAIROS:

Some of you birds had better get on the balls
and board this crate.

IRIS:

Board me? I never
heard such a thing!

106

PISTHETAIROS:

Well, you heard it now.
We'll give you something to squawk about.

IRIS:

Well, really!

PISTHETAIROS:

All right, all right. What gate did you come through?

IRIS:

How should I know? Gates mean nothing to me.

PISTHETAIROS:

Oh. So that's the way it is.

—Well, then,
did you report to the Chief Jackdaw? Say something!
Did you get your passport countersigned by the Storks?
You did not?

IRIS:

Are you in your right mind?

PISTHETAIROS:

Not a single
bird there punched your card for you?

IRIS:

No, or punched
anything else for me, you poor idiot.

PISTHETAIROS:

So
you're flying over foreign territory
without any papers.

107

IRIS:

How else should gods fly?

PISTHETAIROS:

Good God, how should I know?

But they can't do it here!
I don't care if you're a whole fleet of Irises;
you've committed a violation, and the penalty
for that is death.

IRIS:

Mortal, I am immortal.

PISTHETAIROS:

Death just the same!

Things have come to a pretty pass
if we set up a system of border controls, only to have
you gods flying back and forth whenever you feel like it.
But tell me:
What was the destination you had in mind?

IRIS:

Destination? I am about my Father's business.
He has commanded me to remind mankind
that they must sacrifice to the eternal gods,
smiting the hornèd beasts upon their altars
and filling their streets with the smoke of immolation.

PISTHETAIROS:

What do you mean? Sacrifice to what gods?

IRIS:

Why, to us gods in Heaven.

PISTHETAIROS:

So you are gods too?

IRIS:

Can you think of others?

PISTHETAIROS:

I am thinking of the Birds.
So far as mankind is concerned, Birds are now gods.
It's they must have sacrifices—not God, by God!

IRIS:

Alas, deluded worm, think not to stir
the guts of wrath eterne: else heavenly Justice,
with Zeus's pitchfork arm'd, drops from on high
to man's undoing and leaves not a rack
behind. Fried and consumèd shalt thou be,
as i' th' Euripidean Tragedy!

PISTHETAIROS:

Madam, wipe the foam from your mouth,
and do stop quivering so. Am I a slave,
some Lydian or Phrygian slave, that you imagine
you scare me with talk of this kind?

As for Zeus:
you can inform your Zeus
that if he gets in my way I'll burn him out,
yea, I will blast him in Amphíon's hall
with eagles lightningbeak'd that heed my call.
Notify him furthermore
that I command a squadron of six hundred

sky-scaling porphyrion birds in panther skin.
That will hold him, I think: a single Porphyrion once
kept him busy enough.

                    —And if *you* get in my way,
Iris or no Iris, messenger or whatever you are,
I'll just hoist up your legs and get in between:
then, by God, you can tell your wondering friends
how you met an old battleship with a triple prow!

IRIS:

No gentleman would address a lady so.

PISTHETAIROS:

On your way! Scat!

IRIS:

                    I shall certainly tell my Father.

PISTHETAIROS:

Next time, consume someone your own age!

[*Exit* IRIS *in the* machina

CHORUS:

                    My word is sure: [ANTISTROPHE
                    Children of Zeus,
                    No entrance here!
                    And it shall stand.
                    Let no man dare
                    Cajole the skies
                    With ritual brand
                    Or sacrifice.

PISTHETAIROS:

Speaking of mankind, I am worried about our herald.
It's strange that his commission should keep him so long.

[*Enter a* HERALD, *in haste*

HERALD:

O Pisthetairos! O Blessedest! O Sagaciousest!
O Superlativest! O Sagaciousest! O Perspicaciousest!
O Thrice Blessedest! O And-so-forth!

PISTHETAIROS:

Did you speak?

HERALD:

I crown you with this golden crown, the gift
of your admiring public.

PISTHETAIROS:

I thank you.
Tell me: Why does mankind admire me?

HERALD:

O Pisthetairos, mighty father of
Cloudcuckooland the Beautiful, how slight
your skill in understanding human thought
if you must ask that question!

What is man?
Or, rather, what was man before your triumph?
An abject Spartomaniac—long hair,
infrequent baths, bad honest food, knobbly
accessories, the Sokratês pose.

111

What is man now?

Mad about birds! Birds, birds, from the moment
they get out of nest in the morning: eggs and birdseed
for breakfast, and then bird business,
reeding and piping till clucking-off time.
They even affect bird names:
'Partridge' is any man gone in one leg;
Menippos is 'Swallow'; Opountios,
'Monocle de Mon Oncle'; Philoklês
is 'Lark'; Theogenês, 'Gypsy Goose'; Lykourgos,
'Ibis'; Chairephôn, 'Bats'; Syrakosios, 'Jaybird';
and Meidias, of course, is called 'Goon Quail'—
one look at that bashed-in face of his
will tell you why.
                        As for song-writing,
you can't so much as buy a hearing unless
you stuff your lyrics with assorted wild ducks
and swallows, or doves, or geese, or maybe
a few last feathers from a cast-off wing.

That's what it's like down there. And mark my words:
you'll soon be getting visitors by the thousands,
all sorts of men begging to be fitted out
with wings and beaks and claws. Take my advice
and lay in a pile of pinions.

PISTHETAIROS:

                        Heavens, yes!

112

[*1308-1325*]

I can see we'll be busy.

—Quick, you:

[*To a* SERVANT

fill every last basket you can find with wings
and tell Manês to bring them out to me here.
I want to be prepared for these gentlemen.

CHORUS:

My City is Cloudcuckooland,   [STROPHE
    And men of every nation
Confer on us, I understand,
    Ecstatic approbation.

PISTHETAIROS:

And surplus population.

CHORUS:

What wonder though it should be so?
    Here Love and Wisdom dwell,
And through the streets the Graces go,
    And Peace contrives her spell.

PISTHETAIROS:

The servant problem's hell!

CHORUS: [ANTISTROPHE
Manês, awake! New wings, new beaks!

113

Surely there never was
A slower slave. Your master speaks!
The precious moments pass!

[*Enter* MANES *emptyhanded*

PISTHETAIROS:

This Manês is an ass.

[*Exit* MANES

CHORUS:

Wings make the man; let each man wear
The crest that suits his bent:
Musician, merchant, privateer,
Cleric, or laic gent,

[*Re-enter* MANES *as before*

PISTHETAIROS:

Or slave of snail descent.

Manês, I swear by All Hawks, I'll haul you
hairless if you don't get busy! Come on; service!

[*General confusion.* MANES *and other servants appear
and reappear carrying wings of all shapes and sizes.
These are arranged on a bench.*

114

PARRICIDE [*within, singing*]:

  'Ah that the eagle's eager wings were mine,

  To gyre above the waste of bloomless brine!'

PISTHETAIROS:

  That messenger seems to have been right.

  Here comes somebody singing about eagles.

[*Enter a young* PARRICIDE

PARRICIDE:

  Here we are!

  I vow, there's nothing like flying.

                       —Sir,

  I'm mad about birds, I'm

  always up in the air. More than that,

  I apply for citizenship under your laws.

PISTHETAIROS:

  What laws? We Birds have many laws.

PARRICIDE:

  All of them; especially that glorious statute

  that gives Birds the right to strangle their own fathers.

PISTHETAIROS:

  We *do* consider it a sign of manliness

  when a chick stands up to his father and faces him down.

PARRICIDE:

  Exactly my own motive in emigrating:

  I propose to throttle the old man for his property.

PISTHETAIROS:

At the same time we have an ancient decree
(you'll find it in the Book of Storks) that says:
STORKLINGS CARED FOR BY THE STORK THEIR
    SIRE
AND BY HIM TAUGHT TO FLY SHALL IN THEIR
    TURN
CARE FOR THE STORK THEIR SIRE IN HIS OLD AGE.

PARRICIDE:

What was the use of my coming all this distance
if I've got to support my father after all?

PISTHETAIROS:

Come, it's not so bad.
You obviously mean well, and we'll make
a decent orphan bird of you yet, young man.
But first
permit me to recite a useful thought
        'that was given me
        at my mother's knee':
Sons, don't beat your fathers. It's unkind.

> [*During the following speech* PISTHETAIROS *arms the*
> PARRICIDE *with a toy sword, shield, and helmet.*

Stick out your hand: receive this bright cock-spur.
Your other hand: receive this shining wing.
Stick out your neck: receive this crested helm.
Now you're in the Army, cock.

116

Keep awake on guard duty, live on your pay, and let
your father alone. If you feel like fighting,

take a trip to Thrace: there's always a war on there.

PARRICIDE:

You're right. I'll do it, by God!

[*Exit*

PISTHETAIROS:

By God, you'd better!

[*Enter the dithyrambic poet* KINESIAS

KINESIAS [*singing*]:

'Lifted aloft on wings of song,
    Towards high Olympos winging—'

PISTHETAIROS:

This man needs wings if ever a poet did!

KINESIAS [*singing*]:

'Pure in mind, in body strong,
    Ever of thee, love, singing—'

PISTHETAIROS:

Kinêsias, as I live. Old limpety-lop,

why did your limping feet bring you up here?

KINESIAS [*singing*]:

'I aim, nor shall my purpose fail,
    To be a Neo-Nightingale.'

PISTHETAIROS:

Damn your aim. I suppose you can talk sense?

KINESIAS:

Oh, ay. Enwingèd, man, by thee I'd be,
that from the gravid clouds I may charm down
a meed of music for my sacred soul,
  'Batter'd by ev'ry wind that blows,
  And snow'd upon by snowing snows.'

PISTHETAIROS:

This meed of music: you find it in the clouds?

KINESIAS:

Yea, i' the clouds my Muse doth perch and preen.
Wottest thou not that th' dithyrambic gene
burns in the air, most dark, and bright with gloom?
Plastic with pinions, too.

                    I'll give you an example.

PISTHETAIROS:

Never mind.

KINESIAS:

                    No trouble at all. For instance,
here's a description of the upper air:
  Pteroid shapes
  Thro' th' aether traipse,
  Longneck'd wrynecks—

PISTHETAIROS:

Hard alee!

KINESIAS:

  Zigging upon the zagging blast,
  Free in the vast anemoplast—

118

PISTHETAIROS:

By God, I'll free your blast!

KINESIAS:

Free to fly at the wind's behest,
Now north, now south, now east, now west:
Furrowing with my feather'd feet
Those fields where eagles eagles meet,
Praying a blessing on thy name,
Old Architect, for this high game.

PISTHETAIROS:

Stop and put on your wings, damn it, your wings!

[*A brief scuffle about the stage*

KINESIAS:

And is it thus thoudst serve a modern poet?
A poet to whom so many tribes lay claim?

PISTHETAIROS:

Let Leotrophidês claim you to train his squabs!

KINESIAS:

Thou mockest me, proud Patriarch. Farewell.
These wings I'll flap, high water come or hell.

[*Exit* KINESIAS. *Enter an* INFORMER, *singing, unnoticed*
at first in the confusion of the poet's departure

INFORMER:

'What birds are these whose patchwork dress
Reveals that they are penniless?
O Swallow, Swallow, tell me.'

PISTHETAIROS [*aside*]:

That Kinêsias was a rough customer.

—And, by God,

here comes another one!

INFORMER:

'O Swallow, Swallow, tell me.'

I repeat.

PISTHETAIROS:

He seems to be singing about his coat.

Can't blame him: it would take more than one swallow
to make that bearable.

INFORMER:

A little service, please!

Who's distributing wings here?

PISTHETAIROS:

Just step this way.

Now then: what do you want?

INFORMER:

Wings, man, wings.

You deaf?

PISTHETAIROS:

I suppose you're in a hurry
to get to a clothier's.

INFORMER:

Wrong. Plumb wrong.

I am a process-server for the Islands.
Also an Informer.

PISTHETAIROS:

Thanks for the information.

INFORMER:

Also a professional accuser. So I need some wings.

Great thing for this Island Circuit. Big business.

PISTHETAIROS:

A pair of wings will make your business bigger?

INFORMER:

Couldn't. But the pirates, you know: always hanging around.

With wings I could fly right over them like a crane,

belly full of lawsuits for ballast.

PISTHETAIROS:

Of course you could.

Tell me: are you good at spying on aliens?

INFORMER:

Well, a man's got to live. I never learned how to work.

PISTHETAIROS:

Aren't there enough honest jobs in the world,

that a healthy man like you

must pick up money selling false information?

INFORMER:

Wings I came for, not sermons.

PISTHETAIROS:

I just gave you wings.

INFORMER:

The devil you did. All you've done is talk.

PISTHETAIROS:

Haven't you ever heard of 'wingèd words'?

INFORMER:

Wingèd words?

PISTHETAIROS:

Yes, or wingèd actions?
Say you go into a barber's. Well, they're all
sitting around there, swapping lies
about their sons and grandsons. 'I swear to God,'
one of them says,
'I don't know what to make of that boy of mine.
'The horses have got him. Can't keep his feet on the ground.'
Another one says, 'That's nothing.
'Mine wants to take a flier at writing plays.
'The tragic bug's bitten him.'

INFORMER:

So you think
words can make wings?

PISTHETAIROS:

That's it exactly.
Words heighten concepts; words raise a man
out of himself. You came to me for wings:
all right, you can have them; and, what's more,
I'll throw in a word or two of good advice
about getting a job that you won't have to blush for.

INFORMER:

No good. No good at all.

PISTHETAIROS:

Why not?

INFORMER:

Family pride. Can't let the old name down.
There's been Informers in our family
since I don't know when.

—But come:
give me a couple of good swift wings, I don't care
what model, and I'll get back,
denounce a few aliens, get them indicted here,
and then I'm off.

PISTHETAIROS:

You mean you'll have these men
indicted before they get a chance to appear?

INFORMER:

You said it.

PISTHETAIROS:

And while they're on their way to court
you'll swoop down on the Islands and grab their goods?

INFORMER:

You get the idea. I'm busy as a top.

PISTHETAIROS: [*Takes a long whiplash from the bench*
Top? Here's something to make tops spin:
first-class goods from Korkyra.

INFORMER:

Put it away!

PISTHETAIROS:

Call it a pair of wings. By God, it'll send *you*
into a nose-dive!

[*Lashes him*

INFORMER:

Stop it! Police! Stop it!

[*Exit* INFORMER

PISTHETAIROS:

All of a flap, hey? Can't wait around? Too bad!
You sneaking patriot,
this time you pay the court costs!

[*To his attendants*

Come,
let's gather up these wings and go inside.

[*Exit, followed by attendants carrying the bench,
wings, and the rest of the paraphernalia*

CHORIKON:
CHORAL INTERLUDE

CHORUS: [STROPHE

    Numberless are the world's wonders, and we
    Have roosted on most of them. In wicked Thrace
    There grows the remarkable Kleonymos tree,
    Immense, heart-rotted, that in summer yields
    Informative fruit; but in winter time its grace
    Forsakes it, and its boughs shed unused shields.

    And we have seen a region of the dead   [ANTISTROPHE
    Where men with Heroes dine before nightfall,
    But where the reveller walks home in dread
    Lest from the shades a new Orestês come,
    Accost him at the turning of the wall,
    Strip him, beat him, and leave him bare and numb.

SCENE

[*Enter* PROMETHEUS, *muffled from head to foot in a red and yellow cloak and carrying a large black open umbrella.*

PROMETHEUS:

I hope to God Zeus can't see me!

—Pisthetairos!

Where's Pisthetairos?

[*Re-enter* PISTHETAIROS

PISTHETAIROS:

What's going on here?

Who are you in the blankets?

PROMETHEUS:

Look:

is any god following me?

PISTHETAIROS:

God? No.

Who are you?

PROMETHEUS:

Can you give me the correct time?

PISTHETAIROS:

Noon. Maybe a little later. But who
are you?

PROMETHEUS:

Noon, you said?

PISTHETAIROS:

Oh, for God's sake!

PROMETHEUS:

What's the weather like?

PISTHETAIROS:

Hey?

PROMETHEUS:

I said, 'What's

the weather like?'

PISTHETAIROS:

Go to hell!

PROMETHEUS:

Splendid. I'll just

take off these cerements.

[*Throws off the cloak and stands revealed in scarlet tights*

PISTHETAIROS:

Well, I'll be damned! Prometheus!

PROMETHEUS:

Sh, sh, keep your voice down!

PISTHETAIROS:

What's the matter?

PROMETHEUS:

Just don't mention my name. If Zeus finds me here
he'll scalp me. You don't know the half of it.

132

I'll tell you; only,
please hold this umbrella over my head
so the gods can't look down and see me from up there.

PISTHETAIROS:

The same old Prometheus! All right; get under,
and begin to talk.

PROMETHEUS:

Listen.

PISTHETAIROS:

    I am.

PROMETHEUS:

        Zeus is through.

PISTHETAIROS:

                Since when?

PROMETHEUS:

Since you organized Cloudcuckooland.
There's not been so much as a sniff of sacred smoke
coming up to us from a single human altar.
I swear, we're hungrier
than a Thesmophoria fast-day; and, what's worse,
the damnedest lot of starving yowling gods
from the back country are talking about revolt
if Zeus doesn't manage to get a decent consignment
of sacrificial cuts to keep us going.

PISTHETAIROS:

Do you mean to tell me the Barbarians
have gods of their own?

PROMETHEUS:

What about Exekestidês?

Doesn't he have to pray to something?

PISTHETAIROS:

I see.

But these godforsaken gods: what are they called?

PROMETHEUS:

Triballians.

PISTHETAIROS:

Tribal totems.

PROMETHEUS:

I suppose so.

—But this is what I have come down to tell you:
Zeus and these Triballians
are sending a delegation to look into
what's going on here. Take my advice:
laugh at every offer they make to you
until they swear to restore the Birds to power
and give you Basileia for a wife.

PISTHETAIROS:

Basileia? Who is this Basileia?

PROMETHEUS:

She's the prettiest girl you ever saw:
manages Zeus, takes care of his thunderbolts
and all the rest of his weapons—sagacity,
legislation, rearmament, ideology, ultimatums,
revenue officers, jurymen—

134

PISTHETAIROS:

                              She does all that?

PROMETHEUS:

That's only an outline. When you get Basileia,
you've got everything.

                              I thought I ought to tell you:
I have a certain stake in humanity.

PISTHETAIROS:

A well-broiled one, thanks to your foresightedness.

PROMETHEUS:

And I hate the gods.

PISTHETAIROS:

                              And the gods hate you.

PROMETHEUS:

Yes. I'm a regular Timôn.

                              —But it's late.
I must be getting back.

                              Give me my umbrella:
Zeus will think I'm a Virgin of the Escort.

PISTHETAIROS:

Take this footstool with you; it will make a better effect.

                                                    [*Exeunt*

CHORIKON:
CHORAL INTERLUDE

CHORUS:

There is a mystic river   [STROPHE
  In the land of the Shadowfeet
Where Sokratês the Bathless calls
  The souls of men to meet.

There Chickenheart Peisandros
  Made sacrifice one day
To conjure up his own dim soul
  And hear what it would say.

Odysseus-like he cut the throat
  Of a kind of camel-cat;
But all he raised was the squeaking ghost
  Of Chairephôn the Bat.

SCENE

[*Enter the Ambassadors from Olympos:* POSEIDON, HERAKLES, *and a* TRIBALLIAN GOD. *The first wears a sea-weed crown, a cloak embroidered with large horse-heads, and carries a trident and a rigid stuffed fish; the second wears a lion skin and carries a club; the third, blackface, wears a stovepipe hat and is desperately entangled in a multicoloured cloak.*

POSEIDON:

So this is Cloudcuckooland. Very well,
let us proceed to act like a Delegation.

[*To the* TRIBALLIAN

You, there,
what are you up to now? Don't you know better
than to drape your cloak on the left side? Look,
you celestial rustic, it ought to hang on the right,
gracefully, like this. Do you want these people
to take you for Laispodias? Hold still,
can't you? There!
Democracy, what sins are committed in thy name!
Damn it, of all the barbarous gods I've met
you're the barbarousest.
                    —What's your plan, Heraklês?

HERAKLES:

You heard what I said. Just croak the guy
what shut the gods out with this here Stone Curtain.

POSEIDON:

Yes, my good fellow; but we're supposed to discuss peace.

HERAKLES:

All the more reason for croaking him, I say.

> [*Enter* PISTHETAIROS *attended by various birds in kitchen costume; he elaborately disregards the Ambassadors.*

PISTHETAIROS:

                                        Quick, now,
let's have the cheesegrater. Where's the horseradish?
Grate that cheese, somebody. Keep the fire hot.

POSEIDON:

In the name of the Divine Authority,
three gods greet thee, O Man.

PISTHETAIROS:

                        The horseradish.

HERAKLES:

Say, Mac, what kind of a roast is that?

PISTHETAIROS:

Bird roast. Subjects condemned for subversion
of the Authority of the Birds.

HERAKLES:

                        And you use

horseradish?

144

PISTHETAIROS:

Why, it's Heraklês! Good
afternoon, Heraklês.

POSEIDON:

The Divine Authority
empowers three gods to consider conciliation.

A COOK:

Oil's out. What do I do now?

HERAKLES:

No oil?
Damn bad. You can't barbecue without oil.

POSEIDON:

Regarded disinterestedly, this war
subserves no aim of the Divine Authority.
Similarly, your Delegates should reflect
how much you have to gain from a friendly Olympos:
I instance only
fresh rain water for your swamps, and halcyon days.
Shall we initiate talks?

PISTHETAIROS:

I don't see why.
In the first place, we were not the ones
who started hostilities. But let that pass.
As for peace, we are perfectly willing to agree
if the gods will meet our terms. We demand
restoration of our ancient sovereignty
and the return of the sceptre to the Birds.

Let Zeus accept that much, and I'll invite
all three of you to dinner.

HERAKLES:

I vote Yes.

POSEIDON:

You gastric monomaniac, would you vote away
your own Father's crown?

PISTHETAIROS:

That's a silly question.
Do you gods imagine that you will be losing power
by delegating the imperium of the skies?
Surely you know that all over the earth
men are hiding under clouds and breaking your laws
with impunity. Suppose you had the Birds
on your side: then if a man swore
by Zeus and the Crow, say, and broke his oath,
we'd simply have a Crow swoop down upon him
and peck out his right eye.

POSEIDON:

Good, by Myself!

HERAKLES:

I think so too.

PISTHETAIROS [*to* TRIBALLIAN]:

What do *you* say?

TRIBALLIAN:

Wockle.

146

HERAKLES:

The poor fish says Yes.

PISTHETAIROS:

And here's something else.
Suppose a man promises an offering
to some god or other, and maybe greed
gets the better of him, and he thinks: *Well,*
the gods are used to waiting:

we birds
will know how to handle him.

POSEIDON:

How? Instruct me.

PISTHETAIROS:

Well, say that man's
sitting in his office some day, counting his money,
or say he's in the tub enjoying a nice hot bath:
down comes one of the Kites when he isn't looking
and zooms off to Olympos with a couple of his sheep.

HERAKLES:

I say it again: give the Birds what they ask for.

POSEIDON:

What do *you* think?

PISTHETAIROS:

Speak, you divine Mistake.

TRIBALLIAN:

Treeballs beetee gnaw ouch, Glapp.

147

HERAKLES:

He says Yes.

POSEIDON:

If you say so. I suppose I must say so too.

Very well. Divine Authority cedes the Sceptre.

PISTHETAIROS:

Hold on! I nearly forgot.

The Birds are prepared to confirm Zeus' right to Hêra,
but in return

they insist upon my having Basileia.

POSEIDON:

I can see that you are not interested in peace.

Good-bye.

PISTHETAIROS:

It makes no difference to me.

—Now this gravy, cook: see that it's thick enough.

HERAKLES:

Hey, damn it, Admiral, hold on, what the hell?

Who wants to fight a war for a damn woman?

POSEIDON:

What else can we do?

HERAKLES:

Damn it, make peace!

POSEIDON:

Idiot, can't you see he's trying to ruin you?

And you walk right into the trap.

                              Think a moment: if Zeus
gives the Birds what they ask for, and then dies—
Where are you then? Where's your inheritance?

PISTHETAIROS:

Heraklês, don't listen to the man.
Every word he speaks is a delusion.

                                        [*Beckons him aside*

Step over here a minute.
                    —My poor fellow,
that Ancient Mariner is just leading you on.
You inherit from Zeus? You couldn't, not a penny.
You, being a bastard—

HERAKLES:

                    Me, a bastard?

Say, listen, you—

PISTHETAIROS:

                    Well, your mother
was an alien, wasn't she? Besides, Athenê
is heir apparent, and how could she be that
if she had legitimate brothers?

HERAKLES:

                              What if the Boss
says I'm his heir, bastard or no bastard?

PISTHETAIROS:

Illegal. And suppose he does:

                    149

Poseidôn will be the first to contest the will,
as the decedent's brother.

Here is the law,

straight from Solôn:

A BASTARD SHALL NOT INHERIT IF THERE BE
LEGITIMATE ISSUE. IF THERE BE NO LEGITI-
MATE ISSUE, THE PROPERTY SHALL PASS TO
THE NEXT OF KIN.

HERAKLES:

So I can't get nothing out of the Old Man's estate?

PISTHETAIROS:

Nothing at all.

—For that matter,

has your Father enrolled you yet?

HERAKLES:

No. I guess I know why.

PISTHETAIROS:

Come, what's the use of snapping at empty wind?
Join the Birds:

you'll live like a king and feed on pie in the sky.

[*They return to the others.*

HERAKLES:

About that dame we were beating our gums about:
I said, and I say it again: Give him what he wants.

PISTHETAIROS:

You, Poseidôn?

POSEIDON:

No.

PISTHETAIROS:

Then the Triballian
must break the tie. Vote, heavenly Hayseed!

TRIBALLIAN:

Quiffing gamsel cockitty, gotta tweet tweet.

HERAKLES:

He says Yes.

POSEIDON:

I doubt very much if he says Yes
or anything else that matters. But let it pass.

HERAKLES:

He's ready to pass her over, anyhow.

POSEIDON:

Have it your way, you two. Make your peace,
and I'll hold mine.

HERAKLES:

These here top-level talks
are all over, and we say he gets the green light.
Come on, man, you got a date up in the sky
with Basileia and any other damn thing you want.

PISTHETAIROS:

It's a lucky thing that I had these roasts ready.
They'll do for the wedding.

HERAKLES:

You birds run along:

I'll stick around here and keep an eye on the cook.

POSEIDON:

Can't you rise superior to food? You come with us.

PISTHETAIROS:

And somebody bring along my wedding clothes.

[*Exeunt omnes; manet* CHORUS

CHORIKON:
CHORAL INTERLUDE

CHORUS:

Phonéya is that far country   [ANTISTROPHE
   Where the Englottogasters dwell:
They plough the fields there with their tongues
   And sow and reap as well.

Oh blest Englottogasters!
   And yet we need not roam
In search of tongues as versatile—
   They twitch for us at home:

The tongue that tells for ready cash,
   The slimy tongue that smiles,
The paid, applauded, patriot tongue
   That guards us, and defiles.

ÉXODOS

[*Enter* THIRD MESSENGER

MESSENGER:

Thrice happy generation of Birds, O winged
with joy beyond words' contriving: receive
your great Prince in his palace of delight!
His glory burns: no star
flames brighter in the wheeling vault, no sun
has ever blazed so pure. He comes,
and beauty walks beside him crowned
with lightning from God's hand, his divine
Bride, veiled i' th' smoke of incense rising.
Your King, your Queen!
Sing them a song of the Nine Sisters' devising.

> [*Re-enter* PISTHETAIROS, *splendidly gowned, with newly
> gilded wings; he is accompanied by* BASILEIA, *in cloth
> of gold, crowned, her face hidden by a veil.*

CHORUS:

Back!
    Make way there!
        Circle them!
           Dance!
Beat on the bright ground with quick feet
For the Prince of Luck, for his Bride—
  Oh sweet! Oh fair!—
Dance, dance the marriage in the air.

CHORAGOS:

 Dance in the sky,
    joy in the sky!
 Dance in the reign of the Birds,
      dance in
 The augury of his polity:
 Dance Hymen
    the wedding chorus
       dance

CHORUS:

  When heavenly Hêra was the bride   [STROPHE
   Of Zeus in his high hall,
  The Fatal Ladies danced and sang
   This for their festival:
    Round the royal pair we go:
    Hymen O! The wedding O!

  Erôs flicked his golden wings   [ANTISTROPHE
   To be their charioteer,
  And through the swaying skies their car
   Darted in sweet career.
    Round the royal pair we go:
    Hymen O! The wedding O!

PISTHETAIROS:

 For your songs, for your good wishes, thanks:
 I am gratified, and I am sure

that I speak for my wife as well. I should be
even more gratified to hear you perform
two or three odes in honour of my triumph
over the dangerous thunderbolts of Zeus,
the difficult lightning.

CHORUS:

O fire lancing the black night,   [EPODE
  O rage of voices under ground,
Thunder, hurly of rain, bright
  Tempest of sound:
Sing, sing his audacity
  Who draws down from God's throne
God's Basileia, Sovereignty,
  And crowns her his own.
    Round the royal pair we go:
    Hymen O! The wedding O!

PISTHETAIROS:

Follow the bridal, follow, fortunate friends,
to the high lands of God, to the happy bed.
And oh my darling, take
my wings in your shining hands, and I
will lift you, lift you above the sky
in the Birds' dance, the whirring dance.

CHORUS:

Iô! Iô!

Iê Paián! Alalaí!
See the conquering hero go!
Hymen O! The wedding O!

GENERAL NOTES
AND
INDEX OF PROPER NAMES

GENERAL NOTES

Σ = Scholiast

Persons Represented: The Protagonist's name is in doubt. 'Peisthetairos', attested by most of the MSS., is unsatisfactory; of various other forms, 'Pisthetairos'—'trusty friend'—seems to be the best.

3: The scene is deliberately vague. Although Pisthetairos and Euelpidês have come on foot from Athens, the site of the future Cloudcuckooland seems neither terrestrial nor aerial: a dream region, suitable for a dream city. If the transformed King Tereus has chosen to remain in the country that he ruled as a man, the location is Thrace—northward, at any rate, in the direction of witchcraft and delusion.

4: Tereus was a king of Thrace who violated Philomelê, the sister of his wife Proknê, and tore out her tongue so that she should not tell. The sisters avenged themselves by cooking Itys, Tereus' infant son, and serving him up to his father at dinner. The gods' criticism of this Faulknerian episode took the form of changing all three agonists into birds: Tereus became a Hoopoe, Proknê a Swallow, and Philomelê a Nightingale. It is worth noting that A. follows the variant that transforms Proknê, not Philomelê, into the Nightingale. Moreover, she seems to have forgiven Tereus for his affair with her sister, and Tereus has forgotten the dreadful business about Itys. The

165

Nightingale and the Hoopoe are on exemplary domestic terms with each other.

5: A losing war is hard on the national nerves, but A.'s grievance against Athens is that of any intelligent citizen whose government has yielded to fanaticism and public hysteria. Certainly there were traitors and dangerous malcontents in Athens, working for Sparta or for their own interests, but it is also true that the inevitable Informer was providing harmless citizens and defenceless aliens with all too many 'opportunities / to appear in court' on 'loyalty' charges. After the scandals that attended the sailing of the Sicilian Expedition (415 B.C.) professional patriotism had become a golden racket.

10: *The Twelve Gods*: Zeus, Hêra, Poseidôn, Deméter, Hephaistos, Arês, Athenê, Artemis, Aphroditê, Hestia, Apollo, Hermês.

11: *It's Sophoklês' fault*: The reference is to the *Tereus* of Sophoklês, a play no longer extant.

14: *the Red Sea*: 'He means Arabia Felix,' says Σ. Actually he means Cockaigne or Arcady, Bali or Boston, or whatever your personal Eldorado may be.

15: *It's a non-stop honeymoon!*: Bridal wreaths were made of mint leaves and myrtle-berries. Poppy seeds dipped in honey were esteemed as an aphrodisiac and eaten at weddings. The sesame plant was associated with Aphroditê.

21: *gargling in the glade*: The word (ἐπῷζε) is unexpectedly harsh. Pisthetairos is disappointed by the Hoopoe's apparent failure to attract an audience.

23: The *Párodos* is the formal entrance of the Chorus into the *orchestra*, and in *Aves* it is almost entirely spectacle. There is relatively little singing for the Chorus, and the chief interest lies in the costumes of the individual Birds and in the commenting dialogue. Here, as throughout the play, the Choragos is spokesman for the Chorus as a whole.

26: *Bird of Araby*: This is the Cock, the Persian Bird, here called *Mêdos*, 'the Median'. (The phallic pun is the same in Greek as in English.)

My 'Araby' is a licence, intended to make the 'camel' more assimilable.

26: *'Kallias : Hipponikos :: Hipponikos : Kallias II'*: The names are *ad hoc,* for illustrative purposes. In ordinary circumstances the grandson takes his grandfather's name. The Hoopoe is explaining the presence on stage of a younger Hoopoe, whom we may call Hoopoe II. Philoklês was a tragic poet of unsavoury reputation (Σ) who plagiarized the *Tereus* of Sophoklês: that is to say, the monstrous cohabitation of Philoklês with Sophoklês' 'Lady' Hoopoe produced Hoopoe II. Kallias, grandson of Kallias I, was a real enough person: dissolute and wasteful ('always getting plucked'), he is best remembered for Plato's making his house the scene of the *Protágoras.*

28: *Magpie,* &c. Some of A.'s birds, in this list and later, are no longer identifiable—'a bird of some sort,' says Σ—; and the translation reflects this uncertainty.

33: *They'll keep the Owl from attacking us*: Athenê invented pottery; hence the Owl, sacred to her, will not attack pots.

34: *related to my wife*: Proknê was the daughter of King Pandiôn of Athens, hence of the same 'tribe' as Pisthetairos and Euelpidês.

35: *National Cemetery*: Here were buried those Athenians who died in battle for their country. The reservation was called Kerameikos, which is 'Pottersville' rather than 'Potter's Field'.

36: *Gettysbird*: The bloodless one-day siege of Orneai (416 B.C.); hence, no one died in that battle. The Greek name makes the pun inevitable.

41: *Monk the Knifeman*: From the disorderly gossip of Σ we gather that this was one Panaitios, a grumpy ugly cutler who had an actively amorous wife. The general purport seems to be: 'You lay off me, and I'll lay off you'. Panaitios' nickname was Pithêkos, 'Monkey'.

43: *Do you see dinner coming?*: Pisthetairos, in accordance with correct procedure at the beginning of an address, has asked for the ceremonial wreath and the lustral water. Euelpidês affects to mistake this for preparation for a formal dinner.

44: *Hyde Lark*: The Greek says that when the Lark's father died he was encephalated, or hidden in the Lark's head—an absurd allusion to the gestation of Athenê. Euelpidês sees a chance for a joke about the place-name Kephalai, which means 'heads'.

46: *to prostrate themselves*: Probably a genuflection (Σ). At any rate it is to be taken literally: the Kite was so greeted as the harbinger of spring. Euelpidês, carrying his market money in his mouth, seems to have genuflected too vigorously.

46: '*Cuckoo! Back to the furrows . . .*': The meaning of the proverb is obscure; *sed latet,* as the Commentators happily remark, *spurci aliquid.*

48: '*Holy Kites!*': Lampôn, possibly because he didn't want to be bound by his oracles, used to confirm them with this diluted oath; or maybe he was one of those mistaken persons who think that 'My Cow!', or something of the sort, avoids the profanity of 'My God!'

50: The attendant or surrogate birds are appropriate. Aphroditê's phalarope is suggested by *phallos*; as a sea god, Poseidôn should have a water bird; cormorants, like Heraklês, are greedy; and it has always been the wren, not the eagle, who is King of the Birds.

50: *the Good Gosh*: Not a softening, like Lampôn's oath noted above, but a whimsical variation: *Zan* for *Zeus.*

53: '*One crow caws down . . .*': A parody of a line of Hesiod (Frag. 50): 'Nine generations lives the cawing crow'. [Σ]

55: *A poor thing of twigs and straw*: The Hoopoe's nest is proverbially filthy, Proknê being a career musician rather than a housewife.

59: PARÁBASIS: At this point the action of the play is suspended while the author, speaking through the Choragos, addresses the audience. The Parábasis proper begins as a parody of the Theogonies, the philosophical accounts of the origin of the gods and the creation of the world; but this tone, which is precariously balanced between the solemn and the bantering, passes into mild topical satire.

62: *Laid a wind-egg*: This is an unfertilized egg, appropriate for the

168

genesis of Love. Σ obscurely alludes to the Ledaian egg from which the Heavenly Twins, Kastor and Polydeukês, were hatched.

63: *Orestês of the Alleys*: This hoodlum with the glorious nickname, who is mentioned again on p. 127, seems to have impressed A. rather deeply. He must also have had a sense of humour, for there is something comic, to the non-participant, in his habit of stripping his victims of all their clothes after robbing them.

63: *You see Bird in everything*: Birds as omens, a fashionable fad.

67: *a full-fledged Horsecock*: An unhappy Aischylean compound, which A. ridicules again in *Ranae*. Aischylos intended it as a kind of heraldic beast, half fowl, half horse, a figurehead for a ship.

71: *'I shot an arrow . . .'*: Pisthetairos quotes a verse from the lost *Myrmidones* of Aischylos, where a wounded eagle recognizes his own feathers on the shaft of the arrow that struck him.

73: *'what boots a mailèd warrior goddess'*: The whole speech parodies a passage from the lost *Meleagros* of Euripidês.

73: *the Pelargic Wall*: This was a part of the fortifications of the Akropolis. The more common name was 'Pelasgic'; 'Pelargic', however, has the advantage of meaning 'Stork [Wall]'.

74: *And fall off the ladder*: There is no authority for assigning this interpolation and the next one to Euelpidês, but surely the conjecture is allowable. Incorporated in Pisthetairos' speech they have no comic force at all.

75: *a leather beak-rest*: The Crow, as *auletês,* or flute accompanist for the singing, would be wearing a leather lip-guard.

76: *Artemis Siskin*: One of the mystical names of Artemis was Kolainis (Σ). The *Akalanthis* is a bird, the siskin. This is straining for a pun; but a pun of sorts emerges.

79: *Author of Aitna*: The Poet's lyrics are a farrago of imperfectly remembered fragments from the standard poets. Here he is mutilating a Pindaric ode on Hiero, Tyrant of Syracuse and founder of the town of Aitna.

96: *Owls of Laureion*: Coins begetting smaller coins; see Index of Proper Names *s.v.* LAUREION.

102: *Egyptian hodcarrier*: A. is thinking of the accounts—Herodotos, for example—of the building of the Pyramids by the slave workmen of Cheops.

102: *Cranes from Libya*: Because of their improbable shape, cranes were supposed to need a ballast of stones in order to fly.

103: *Ah feet . . .*: A proverb; but Pisthetairos substitutes 'feet' for the 'hands' of the original.

109: *Euripidean Tragedy*: 'In the [lost] *Likymnios* of Euripidês, somebody or something gets struck by lightning'. [Σ]

109: *some Lydian or Phrygian slave*: A parody of Euripidês: *Alkestis* 675, Pherês to Admêtos.

111: *An abject Spartomaniac*: It is curious that in a long war it should become fashionable among certain people to ape the manners of the enemy.

111: *the Sokratês pose*: Here, as in the *chorikon* on p. 139, A. reveals his inability to admire the Great Martyr. The full-dress attack takes place in *Nubes,* but even in these minor skirmishes the animus is apparent, and only by shutting our minds to the plain sense of words can we conclude that this is a friendly raillery.

115: *'Ah that the eagle's . . .'*: Σ notes that these verses are quoted [in parody?] from the lost *Oinomaos* of Sophoklês.

116: *a decent orphan bird*: A male war-orphan would be educated by the State. There are vestiges of a dim ornithological pun.

117: *'Lifted aloft . . .'*: Kinêsias enters singing a love-poem by Anakreôn.

118: *Oh, ay. Enwingèd . . .*: The absurd diction parodies the manner of the dithyrambic poets, but there is a serious criticism implied: the poetry of Kinêsias is 'wingèd' not because of its exaltation, but because of its vain triviality (πρὸς τὸ κοῦφον, says Σ).

119: *so many tribes*: Although there may be a comic allusion here to the many cities that claimed Homer as a native son, the central irony is more topical. The office of Choragos, or Trainer of the Chorus for the dramatic festivals, was important and much sought after. A. suggests that Kinêsias, a vapid poet, would be much in demand among the various tribes competing at the festivals, but that no one could have a better claim to his services as Choragos than Leotrophidês, himself a silly unsubstantial dramatist.

119: *'What birds are these . . .'*: Parody of a song by Alkaios of Mytilenê.

120: *the Islands*: The Greek Islanders, not being Athenians, would be easy prey for the Informer.

121: *belly full of lawsuits*: For the cranes' ballast, see note on p. 102.

121: *I never learned how to work*: See Luke 16:3: *Ait autem vilicus intra se: Quid faciam quia dominus meus aufert a me vilicationem? fodere non valeo, mendicare erubesco.*

125: CHORIKON: In this short ode the Birds begin to describe the strange places that they have seen in their migrations. The Thracian tree stands for the recreant bully Kleonymos, the shed 'unused shields' representing his own shield, disgracefully thrown away in battle. Kleonymos made part of his living as a paid informer: the money would come in during the summer sessions, slack off during the winter. The Antistrophe, which at first sight seems to change the subject, actually pursues it. Kleonymos is being equated with the notorious bandit Orestês (see note on p. 63), while, at the level of myth, he becomes a kind of burlesque Aigisthos accosted by Agamemnon's avenging son: the double allusion enforces a shift in the point of view. Σ explains 'numb' by recalling that a chance encounter with a Hero (the bandit had an heroic nickname) was supposed to paralyze one's side.

134: *Basileia*: Her name means Sovereignty, Imperium. She has no place in the official Pantheon, but is an *ad hoc* creation to provide Pisthetairos with a mate equivalent to Zeus' Hêra. The final mockery of this drama, of course, is the apotheosis of the bungling Hero.

135: *A well-broiled one*: Prometheus first taught men the use of fire.

135: *Take this footstool*: At the Panathenaia Festival the daughters of Athenian aristocrats were attended by wealthy girls of foreign ancestry who carried ceremonial footstools and parasols. Prometheus hopes that Zeus, looking down from Olympos, will mistake him for one of these attendants.

137: CHORIKON: The Birds' travel lecture proceeds. The Shadowfeet were a remarkable tribe, said to live in Libya, who enjoyed feet so large that they could be used as parasols during siesta time. This is a fit setting for the deplorable Sokratês, who is represented as 'leading the souls of men'—leading them, that is to say, as Odysseus did the souls in Hadês, but also misleading them by perverse teaching, a charge that A. constantly makes against this philosopher. The Strophe is a comic *Nekuia*, parodying the eleventh book of the *Odyssey*. The fainthearted Peisandros, having lost his own soul, goes to the land of the Shadowfeet to conjure it back.

143: *the Ambassadors from Olympos*: This theophany seems outrageous to us, but our ideas of what constitutes blasphemy are different from the Greeks', who would find A. brilliantly but conventionally comic.

143: *Democracy, what sins . . .* : Zeus, to be fair, has decided that even the Barbarians should be represented in this embassage.

144: *The horseradish*: Literally, *silphion*.

146: *by Myself!*: Poseidôn swears 'By Poseidôn!'

146: *Wockle*: The Triballian speaks a murky language rather like that of Muta and Juva in *Finnegans Wake*. Much needless ingenuity has been expended by Professors attempting to reduce it to sense.

148: *Who wants to fight a war for a damn woman?*: As the Trojan War was fought for Helen.

150: *has your Father enrolled you yet?*: In the register of citizens; as the illegitimate son of a foreign woman, Heraklês would be ineligible.

150: *pie in the sky*: The Greek phrase was 'birds' milk', but this seems too esoteric.

153: CHORIKON: The travelogue resumed. The Englottogasters, 'men who live by their tongues', are nearer home than the Shadowfeet:

they are to be found wherever men make money by informing on their fellows, and are particularly flagrant in times of political uncertainty.

157: ÉXODOS: The conclusion of the play is dictated not only by dramatic appropriateness—the marriage and deification of the Hero—, but by ritual inheritance. Comedy culminates in marriage, and the final scene (*cf.* the *Pax* and, though slightly different in vein, the *Lysistrata*) has overtones of an ancestral fertility rite. The Chorus sings of the wedding of Zeus and Hêra, thus equating Pisthetairos and Basileia with the King and Queen of Heaven. The ordinary man has found Cloudcuckooland, his Utopia, and now becomes God. Like God, he insists upon the recital of his own meritorious exploits.

162: *Iê Paián!*: The play ends with a volley of ritual phrases, among which rings the Athenian battle-cry, *Alalaí!*, which had been *Eleleú!* among the Birds.

INDEX OF PROPER NAMES

*Arabic numerals in square brackets refer to the
lineation of the Greek text.*

Σ = Scholiast

AESOP, AISOPOS: A semi-legendary writer of fables.

AGAMEMNON: Commander of the Greeks in the Trojan War.

AISCHINES: An impoverished braggart politician; his 'castles' [822] are
what we should call 'castles in Spain'.

AITNA: A town on the slope of the Sicilian mountain, founded by Hiero of
Syracuse.

AKROPOLIS: The Citadel of Athens, sacred to Athenê; here [827] the inner
fortress of Cloudcuckooland.

ALKMENE: A mistress of Zeus; mother of Heraklês.

ALOPE: A mistress of Poseidôn.

AMMON: A famous temple and oracle of Zeus in Libya.

AMPHION: Husband of Niobê; the quotation [1247] is an absurdly jumbled
parody of a passage in the [lost] *Niobê* of Aischylos.

APHRODITE: Goddess of love.

APOLLO: God of healing, of prophecy, of the sun.

ARES: God of war.

ARTEMIS: Goddess of the chase; *see* GENERAL NOTES on p. 169.

174

ATHENE: Daughter of Zeus; tutelary goddess of Athens.
ATHENS: Chief city of the district of Attika.

BABYLON: The Assyrian capital, on the Euphratês River; Herodotos (I:178 *sqq.*) describes its enormous and complex walls.
BAKIS: A celebrated and indefatigable Boiotian soothsayer.
BASILEIA: 'Sovereignty', or 'Empery', personified as a housekeeper of Zeus and, later, the bride of Pisthetairos.
BOIOTIA: A country north of Attika.

CHAIREPHON: An Athenian friend of Sokratês, nicknamed 'Bat' [1296] because of his squeaky voice and sallow complexion.
CHAIRIS: A musician, 'somewhat frigid' according to Σ, who seems to have offended A.'s sense of propriety; here [857] a crow accompanying the Chorus; *see* GENERAL NOTES on p. 169.
CHAOS: A pre-Olympian deity; primal matter.
CHIANS: The Island of Chios supported Athens early in the Peloponnesian War, and a clause for the Chians was accordingly added to prayers for the public good. After the Sicilian Expedition, Chios defected to Sparta.

DAREIOS: King of Persia (549-485 B.C.).
DELPHOI: A famous oracle of Apollo, in Phokis.
DEMETER: Sister of Zeus; goddess of agriculture and vegetation.
DIAGORAS: A native of Mêlos, professor of Philosophy in Athens, accused and condemned *in absentia* for atheism.
DIEITREPHES: A self-made man, manufacturer of wicker baskets, who bought his way into the upper echelons of the Government.
DIONYSOS: God of wine.
DODONA: A notable oracle of Zeus.

ENGLOTTOGASTERS: 'Belly-tongued'; used [1696] of political informers and the officials who employ them.
EPOPS: The Hoopoe, *Upupa epops*; *see* GENERAL NOTES on p. 165.

EREBOS: A pre-Olympian deity; usually, son of Night and Chaos; the infernal depths.

EROS: Son of Aphroditê; god of love.

EURIPIDES: Tragic poet (484-406 B.C.).

EXEKESTIDES: A parvenu alien living in Athens.

GRACES: Aglaia, Thaleia, and Euphrosynê, daughters of Zeus and Aphroditê, goddesses of delight.

HALIMOS: A town in Attika, south of Athens.

HEBROS: A river in Thrace.

HERA: Sister and wife of Zeus.

HERAKLES: Son of Zeus and Alkmenê; most famous of the legendary Heroes; often represented by A. as a gutton and braggart.

HERMES: The winged Messenger of the gods.

HESTIA: Goddess of the hearth; as 'Nestiarch' [865], absurdly assimilated to the Birds.

HIPPONIKOS: An illustrative name; see GENERAL NOTES on p. 167.

HOMER: The epic poet.

HYMEN: God of marriage.

IRIS: The rainbow goddess; confidential messenger of Hêra.

KALLIAS: A wealthy and dissolute Athenian amateur of philosophy. In v. 283 the name is illustrative; see GENERAL NOTES, p. 167.

KARIAN: A native of Karia, a country of Asia Minor. The Karians were said to prefer fighting on mountain tops as offering better opportunities for flight; hence [292-3] the pun on 'crests'.

KINESIAS: A dithyrambic poet of Thebes in Boiotia; he is amusingly attacked by A. in Lysistrata.

KLEISTHENES: An Athenian bravo noted for his effeminacy.

KLEOKRITOS: An effeminate fat man with large feet who looked like an ostrich (Σ).

176

KLEONYMOS: A cowardly officer who became famous for having thrown away his shield in battle; *see* GENERAL NOTES, p. 171.

KOLONOS: A small town, suburb of Athens.

KORINTH: A city on the isthmus between Attika and the Peloponnesos; A. affects to believe that it is inhabited exclusively by lewd wantons.

KORKYRA: The modern Corfù; the 'first-class goods' [1463] are whips, which were manufactured there.

KRANAOS: One of the mythical founder-kings of Athens.

KRIOA: A deme of Attika.

KRONOS: Father of Zeus.

KYBELE: An Asiatic goddess worshiped as *Magna Mater,* the Mother of gods; in *v.* 875 she is the Great Ostrich.

LAISPODIAS: An Athenian general with a limp (Σ), or possibly the reference is to his sexual incapacity (Σ). The Triballian has draped his cloak as though to conceal his left leg—most inelegant behaviour.

LAKONIA: A country of the Peloponnesos; chief city, Sparta.

LAMPON: A noted soothsayer.

LAUREION: A town in Attika famous for its goldmines; the Owl of Athenê was stamped on coins: hence, at *v.* 301 we should say 'coals to Newcastle'.

LEPREON: A town in Elis; the name suggests leprosy.

LEOTROPHIDES: A dithyrambic poet, thin and corpselike in appearance (Σ).

LIBYA: A region of Africa.

LOKRIS: A district of Greece, extending from Thessaly to Boiotia.

LYKOURGOS: 'Called Ibis either because of his Egyptian extraction or because of his skinny legs. There is a redundancy of the ibis in Egypt (Σ)'.

LYSIKRATES: A venal Athenian official.

MANES: Name for a servant.

MANODOROS: Name for a servant.

177

MEGABAZOS: A Persian nobleman, general in the service of King Dareios, *q.v.*

MEIDIAS: A corrupt and perverse politician; 'Quail' seems to have been a cant word in boxing, as we might say 'Punchy', and apparently refers to Meidias' dazed & glazed expression.

MELANTHIOS: A tragic poet, effete & afflicted with leprosy (Σ) or some disease resembling it.

MELIANS: Inhabitants of Mêlos, which, in the year preceding this play, had been blockaded by Nikias and starved into submission.

MENELAOS: Brother of Agamemnon; husband of Helen; one of the Greek commanders at Troy.

METON: A famous astronomer and architect. He opposed the Sicilian Expedition and feigned insanity in order to avoid serving on it.

MUSES: Nine goddesses presiding over the arts and sciences; daughters of Zeus and Mnemosynê ('Memory').

NAUSIKAA: A princess of Phaiakia, daughter of Alkinoös, who befriended Odysseus.

NIKIAS: A prominent and disastrous Athenian commander in the Peloponnesian War.

ODYSSEUS: Wiliest of the Greek chieftains at Troy, and hero of Homer's *Odyssey;* here [1560] the allusion is to his performing the sacrificial rites necessary for summoning up the dead in Hadês (*Od.* XI).

OLOPHYXOS: A town near Mt Athos, in Makedonia. The name was chosen for the sake of a heavy pun.

OLYMPIANS: The gods, as living upon Mt Olympos, *q.v.*

OLYMPIC: Pertaining to the great athletic contests at Olympia.

OLYMPOS: A mountain in Thessaly; seat of the gods.

OPOUNTIOS: A one-eyed grafter; the word is also the proper adjective from Opoûs, *q.v.*

OPOUS: A town in Lokris, *q.v.*

178

ORESTES: Not the long-suffering son of Agememnon, but a foot-pad who assumed the heroic name. *See* GENERAL NOTES on p. 169.

PAN: An Arkadian rural god.

PANDORA: 'The Earth, since it gives us everything necessary to life' (Σ); not to be confused, at any rate, with the Greek equivalent of Eve.

PARIS: Prince of Troy, son of Priam; Aphroditê bribed him to award her the prize in the most notable of all beauty contests.

PEISANDROS: A notoriously craven politician.

PEISIAS' SON: Apparently a traitorous citizen; but the evidence is very vague, in spite of lurid hints by Σ.

PELARGIC WALL: The Stork Wall, *Pelargikon*, of the Akropolis at Athens.

PHALERON: A port of Athens, notable for its sea food.

PHARNAKES: A Persian nobleman operating as an 'enemy agent' in Athens; the Inspector [1028] is in his pay.

PHILEMON: 'Lampooned as a foreigner, and a Phrygian one into the bargain' (Σ).

PHILOKLES: A tragic poet, nicknamed 'Lark'; he wrote a play called *Tereus, or, the Hoopoe,* much of it plagiarized from Sophoklês.

PHILOKRATES: The proprietor of the shop where Euelpidês and Pisthetairos bought their bird guides [*cf.* 13 *sqq.*].

PHOIBOS: An epithet of Apollo.

PHOINIKIA: Phoenicia, a country in Asia Minor.

PHONÉYA: An invented name. The Greek is *Phanês*, the root of which suggests the pseudo-patriot Informers who are supposed to live in that country.

PHRYGIA: A country in Asia Minor.

PHRYNICHOS: A tragic poet, *fl.* 500 B.C.

PINDAR: Lyric poet (522-442 B.C.).

PORPHYRION: One of the Titans in the conflict with Zeus; [1249] the Purple Waterhen, *Porphyrio veterum.*

POSEIDON: God of the sea.

PRIAM: King of Troy.

PRODIKOS: A prominent sophist, reputedly a teacher of Euripidês and Sokratês.

PROKNE: The Nightingale, wife of Tereus, *q.v.*

PROMETHEUS: A son of the Titan Iapetos, and hence a semi-divine being; reputed to have created man and to have stolen fire from Heaven for the comfort of his creation: for both of which acts he was persecuted by Zeus.

PROXENIDES: An irresponsible boaster; he comes from the wholly imaginary town of Kompasai, a word derived from the verb κομπάζω, 'shoot off the mouth'.

PYTHODELIAN: The Swan, sacred to Apollo, takes Apollo's epithets: Pythian, as god of the Delphic Oracle, and Dêlian, as native of Dêlos.

SABAZIOS: A Phrygian god, assimilated to Dionysos.

SAKAS: Popular name for a foreigner aspiring to Athenian citizenship.

'SALAMINIA': A state galley in the Athenian service; at *v.* 147, a kind of glorified police boat.

SARDANAPALOS: A lavish and splendidly dissolute king of Assyria.

SEMELE: A mistress of Zeus; mother of Dionysos.

SIMONIDES: An Ionian poet (556-467 B.C.).

SOKRATES: Philosopher and teacher (469-399 B.C.); see GENERAL NOTES on p. 170.

SOLON: The lawgiver (639-559 B.C.).

SOPHOKLES: Tragic poet (497-405 B.C.).

SOUNION: An Attic promontory and town, site of a temple of Poseidôn.

SPARTA: Chief city of Lakonia.

SPINTHAROS: Lampooned for the same reason as Philêmon, *q.v.*; otherwise unknown.

SPORGILOS: An Athenian barber.

SYRAKOSIOS: A politician; author of a law forbidding the comic poets to introduce real persons into their plays.

TARTAROS: The infernal & punitive depths.

TELEAS: An unstable Athenian, adequately described in his own words quoted in *vv*. 169-170.

TEREUS: A king of Thrace, transformed, for his outrageous behaviour, into a Hoopoe; *see* GENERAL NOTES on p. 165.

THALES: Mathematician and philosopher (*fl*. 590 B.C.).

THEOGENES: A boastful, showy man of largely imaginary wealth.

THESMOPHORIA: A festival of Deméter, celebrated in November; the fourth day was a fast.

THRACE: Roughly, the territory north of the Black Sea.

TIMON: A celebrated Athenian misanthrope.

TITANS: Pre-Olympian divinities who revolted against Zeus and were defeated by him in a battle on the Phlegraian Plain; here [824-5] the great combat is reduced to a riot of boasters.

TRIBALLIANS: A savage Thracian tribe.

XANTHIAS: Name for a servant.

ZEUS: Father of gods and men.

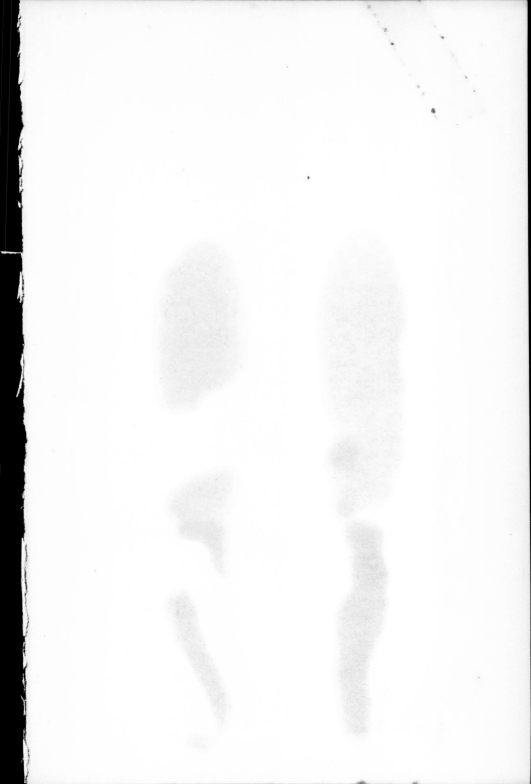

DATE DUE	